THE BRIDGES
OF NEW JERSEY

THE BRIDGES OF NEW JERSEY

PORTRAITS OF GARDEN STATE CROSSINGS

STEVEN M. RICHMAN

RUTGERS UNIVERSITY PRESS

NEW BRUNSWICK, NEW JERSEY, AND LONDON

LIBRARY OF CONGRESS CATALOGING-IN-PUBLICATION DATA

Richman, Steven M., 1955–
    The bridges of New Jersey : portraits of Garden State crossings / Steven M. Richman.
       p.   cm.
    Includes bibliographical references and index.
    ISBN 0–8135–3510–7 (hardcover : alk. paper)
    1. Bridges—New Jersey—History.   2. Bridges—New Jersey—History—Pictorial
works. I. Title.
    TG24.N5R53 2005
    388.1'32'09749—dc22

                                        2004008246

A British Cataloging-in-Publication record for this book is available
from the British Library.

The publication of this volume has been made possible, in part, by a gift from
Nicholas G. Rutgers IV and Nancy Hall Rutgers to support books about New Jersey.

Manufactured in the United States of America

To my children, Justin, Kerry, Alison, and Hannah,
bridges to the future; my parents,
David Richman (deceased) and Sheila Richman,
bridges to the past; and my wife, Jeanne

CONTENTS

COVERED BRIDGES — 91

CANTILEVER BRIDGES — 94

SUSPENSION BRIDGES — 110

MOVABLE BRIDGES 128

GIRDER BRIDGES 147

PREFACE

This book is intended as a testament to the aesthetic and engineering achievements found in the bridges of New Jersey. It is also a personal commentary on this most original, misunderstood, and occasionally peculiar of states. New Jersey is a breathing paradox. Nicknamed the Garden State for its agrarian roots, it is also one of the most densely populated and industrialized of states. Although often mocked and stereotyped in popular American culture, New Jersey boasts some of the finest educational and scientific establishments in the world. We should not forget its citizens' contributions to national and world culture. Not least among these achievements are the state's numerous bridges, making New Jersey a vast open-air museum of "structural art."

According to the New Jersey Department of Transportation Web site, there are 6,337 *highway* bridges alone in New Jersey. Of these, 2,431 are owned by counties, 2,346 by the state, nearly 1,000 by the New Jersey Turnpike and Garden State Parkway authorities, 68 by the Port Authority of New York and New Jersey, and some 55 by the Atlantic City Expressway. One hundred twenty-four are identified as "orphans." Some 2,000 of the state's highway and railroad bridges are of sufficient size to have been surveyed for their historical significance. Numerous other railroad bridges also exist, many of which have been similarly surveyed by New Jersey Transit.

Bridges traverse rivers, streams, railroads, and roadways. Several dozen cross the Delaware River, carrying pedestrian, vehicular, and railroad traffic. Three connect New Jersey to Staten Island. Some date back to the state's colonial era and the Revolutionary War. Others are recognized worldwide for their size or their importance in the annals of engineering. Still others serve as symbols, cherished by their local communities. Remnants of abandoned, decayed, or neglected bridges provide visual links to the state's industrial and social history. Some of those still in use are built of materials that will never be used again, or are of a design no longer considered worth building. They are like the rare survivors of endangered species.

New Jersey is a peninsular state, bordered east and west by the Hudson and Delaware rivers. Other significant rivers—the Raritan, Passaic, and Navesink, to name a few—cut swaths across it, and their tributaries meander throughout the state. Before bridges spanned the state's major rivers, there were ferries. Different regions of the state were brought together by early roads, such as the ones that connected Coryell's Ferry (Lambertville), Trenton, and Burlington in the center and, in the south, linked Burlington to Haddonfield to Gloucester to Raccoon (Swedesboro) to Salem.

Consequently, travelers who wished to continue on to Philadelphia or New York, or to cross where the roads were interrupted, as at the Raritan River in New Brunswick, had to use the local ferry. Such crossings were subject to not only the vicissitudes of weather but also the vagaries of the ferryman, who might be on the other side or "delayed" in one of the taverns that marked the ferry stations. In the period from about 1700 to 1760, according to historian John Cunningham, a trip across New Jersey "required a ferry ride from Philadelphia to either Bordentown or Burlington, followed by a jolting stage wagon ride to the Amboys, and then another long and uncertain ferry trip to New York by way of the Arthur Kill." He later quotes "a traveler" writing in 1793: "[I]f the surgeons of Princeton object to having the roads mended for fear travelers will have no bones broken, they ought to get their bones broken." It would seem that commuter frustration in New Jersey has deep roots.

Although historian Wheaton J. Lane claimed that the colonial officials of New Jersey did not pay much attention to bridge building, and that New Jersey had "few large stone bridges because of their high cost," that situation (if true) seems to have changed by the end of the eighteenth century. Three significant bridges—one in New Brunswick and two in Newark—were constructed in 1795, spanning the Raritan and the Hackensack and Passaic rivers, respectively, and another was completed over the Delaware at Trenton in 1806. Cunningham notes that by 1806, thanks to these bridges, "a traveler could proceed on land or over bridges from Philadelphia to Paulus Hook" or Hoboken.

As stagecoach travel became regularized, and as business and political leaders began to realize that a reliable transportation network was necessary to improve local economies, there was less tolerance for the undependable ferries. And, of course, there was money to be made on bridges. Their oversight and financing were left to local officials. Although toll revenue might recoup the investment, the original funds were raised either by public lottery or by the formation of bridge companies and the sale of stock by subscription. In this way, there was an analogy to the ferries. One obtained a ferry license originally by royal edict, and later by legislative grant. Bridges were also authorized by statute and regulated as well.

As railroads replaced ferries and New Jersey industrialized, population growth in the nineteenth and twentieth centuries expanded, thereby increasing the need for more and larger bridges. New Jersey, positioned between New York and Philadelphia, became a corridor marked by internationally renowned bridges. The state attracted the attention of some of the nation's most prominent engineers, some of whom actually lived or established businesses in New Jersey.

This book highlights sixty of the state's bridges, ranging from the famous to the not-so-famous, which exemplify the diversity of engineering and architectural challenges and achievements. Others of interest are featured in the color supplement. I have sought to capture the aesthetic attraction of these works and, to some extent, the stories behind them and their place in the context of New Jersey (and sometimes American) history and culture. The text is meant to supplement the images, not vice versa. It is my hope that the book will inspire readers to observe the rich variety of engineering and artistic considerations that have gone into these features of the landscape, which are too often taken for granted. In our daily travels, it is worth taking time to understand just how they came to be and what their historic connections are.

In some cases, my choices of which bridges to include may appear a bit eclectic. Over the years, in the course of preparing this book and speaking with many bridge aficionados, I have been struck by how attached people can become to a particular bridge. The process of selection was based on a personal assessment of aesthetics and historical interest. Some bridges, of course, are famous. Others hold a personal appeal, or seem representative of a type, or are simply too important to be ignored. Some bridges deemed by authors of earlier bridge surveys to be significant from a historical, engineering, or political perspective may not be included here, given the limitations of space and my own preferences. In some cases, when a survey's authors indicated a particular bridge to be of statewide, if not national, prominence, I considered it. For example, among the movable bridges, I included the Federal Street Bridge in Camden and substituted the Oceanic Bridge for others that I had found but that apparently were altered enough from their original construction to be judged not historically significant. To those readers who remain chagrined by some exclusions, my apologies.

First and foremost, I intend this to be a visual work. In my photographs I seek to capture the bridges as works of art, and not simply as subjects of documentary photography. I have been intrigued by Professor David Billington's arguments for consideration of bridges as structural art. Yet bridges are also about connection, metaphorical as well as physical. Other connections may by kept alive by the name of a bridge. In this regard, for example, I chose to include the Nevius Street Bridge in Raritan. Although it is significant from an engineering perspective because it is one of the few remaining wrought-iron bridges in excellent condition, my choice was supported by information I found on a genealogy Web site, which traced a Nevius family from Raritan Landing in Somerset County back some five centuries to a Nevius family in Holland. A similar story lies behind the name of the girder bridge at Scudder Falls, also featured, which carries Interstate 95 over the Delaware River.

As a lawyer, I am trained to pursue factual accuracy and carefully cite the source and expression of information. Because there are limited ways in which to convey certain detailed technical information, I often found in my researches that different sources would use almost exactly the same wording. Not uncommonly, factual inaccuracies or discrepancies also carried from source to source, so that at times authorities simply disagreed, or provided different interpretations of theories or even definitions. This is not a new or unique problem. In 1929, in his *Bridges of the World: Their History and Construction*, Charles S. Whitney observed, "There is considerable disagreement among various writers regarding the early history of bridges." In my experience, the same can be said about more modern bridges as well. It has been a revelation to find so much inconsistent information from so many sources, put forward in each as "fact." Even the answers to seemingly straightforward questions, such as the percentage of carbon in wrought and cast iron, differed from one source to another. My purpose has not been to write an exhaustive work detailing the definitive history of each bridge, bridge company, engineer, or bridge design. Rather, it is to provide in one place a solid overview from which the reader may pursue more detailed sources. If, despite my best efforts (to use another lawyer's safeguard), inadvertent errors have crept in, I offer my apologies and welcome comment or correction from knowledgeable readers.

Likewise, I have sought to respect all sources' original expression, giving credit in the text for direct quotations and opinions. Readers seeking more detail are encouraged to consult the sources listed in the bibliography. Many of the books listed there have their own bibliographies and refer to certain older histories of bridges or other specific works that I have not consulted. In the case of Internet sites, it has not been possible to list each one that I searched. Tracing information on some bridges has been like piecing together a mosaic. Sites that provided limited information are not necessarily listed; others referenced may no longer be active. Some articles once available on the Internet may now exist only in their original hard copies. Readers wishing for specific information may contact me at srichman@richmangalleries.com.

It is customary to note that any work such as this is not made in isolation. Assistance and enthusiastic support for the project was offered by the editorial staff of Rutgers University Press; in particular, the advice of editor Melanie Halkias was invaluable. The encouraging work of my copyeditor, Gretchen Oberfranc, caused me to rethink and improve various portions of the text. Marilyn Campbell kept the book on track through production.

I also wish to thank David Koenig, the historian of New Jersey Transit, for supplying information on various railroad bridges; I have included one of his favorites, the railroad bridge known as the North Branch Viaduct. Professor Thomas Booth of Penn State University, one of the team that conducted a survey of Hunterdon County's stone bridges, was extremely generous with his time and knowledge. Dara Calender of the New Jersey Department of Environmental Protection made available New Jersey Transit's bridge survey, and Ginny Baeckler of the Plainsboro Public Library was helpful in locating certain press articles.

I wish to acknowledge my special gratitude to Carla Heymsfeld, my cousin and an author in her own right. Her constant encouragement was particularly welcome in moments of frustration.

THE BRIDGES
OF NEW JERSEY

INTRODUCTION

THE ALLURE OF THE BRIDGE

Each of us has an individual experience and reaction to bridges. There is the immediate pride in the human achievement of erecting something tangible, lasting, and beneficial to humanity. On further reflection, we also recognize that a bridge has positive connotations when used as a metaphor for linking two places, ideas, persons, groups, and so forth. We speak of building bridges to create harmony and working relationships. The notion of a bridge in conversation and in social life is one of strength and importance, of a construction that enables us to cross to a place previously unreachable or, at best, attainable only after considerable effort. As engineer and author Charles S. Whitney wrote in *Bridges of the World* (1929), "Bridges typify progress more than any other structures built by man." Perhaps without realizing it, we feel the sense of connectedness we need and desire as human beings when we look upon the most obvious physical manifestation of something that brings us together.

To appreciate the bridges of New Jersey and gain a deeper understanding of their history, we need to know something about bridges in general. We can begin with the simple definition provided by one of America's first bridge engineers, Squire Whipple (1804–1888). "A Bridge," he wrote in 1847, "is a structure for sustaining the weights of carriages and animals in their transit over a stream, gulf or valley." Thomas Pope, writing his own history of bridges early in the nineteenth century, expanded on this definition and the purpose of a bridge in a way that anticipates the modern metaphor of the bridge as connection:

> That Bridges were requisite in the earliest periods of time, we cannot doubt, from the knowledge we possess of the common operations of nature. Seas, Lakes, Rivers, Brooks, and Swamps, must have existed formerly as well as now; and man, in his common pursuits, must have invented means of surmounting these obstacles to his correspondence with his fellow man, and keeping up the chain of connexion so necessary to his existence, as well as to his gratification.

Most likely, primitive humans first discovered bridges by chance. Perhaps a river carving its way through rock formed a natural bridge, or a vine became tangled in trees on opposite banks, or a tree fell across a stream. The American bridge builder and engineer David Steinman speculated that nature in fact provided the inspiration for the three major types of bridges—the corbelled arch, beam, and suspension bridge—and that prehistoric humans learned from and imitated these naturally occurring features.

Awe-inspiring natural bridges—for example, Landscape Arch and Rainbow Bridge in Arches National Park in Utah—attest to the strength of the arch, and we may reasonably surmise that the first human-constructed bridges were simple structures that followed this pattern observed in nature. The Romans, although not the inventors of the arch (credit goes to the Babylonians), can fairly be said to have successfully exploited its principles. Some of the stone arch bridges built by Roman engineers throughout the once vast empire survive to this day.

In England, evidence remains of primitive "clapper" bridges (from the Latin *claperius*, meaning "pile of stones"). These first beam, or stringer, bridges were formed by laying a flat stone or log on supports without need for complex mathematical calculations or resolution of engineering problems.

By the same token, suspension bridges may have their origins in ropes and vines used for carrying people over ravines and canyons. Perhaps someone first swung from one point to another, and later kept the vine or rope attached to two points so that cargo or persons could slide along from one end to the other. Eventually, these supports would hold another vine or rope over which people could walk, ultimately becoming a "roadway" in itself.

Anthony Flint, in "Some Highlights in the History of Bridge Design," describes the history of bridge engineering as a process of synthesis. Even though advances in construction materials have occurred, the basic structural forms, he contends, have "changed little since early times." For example, the stone arch bridges constructed by Sumerians six thousand years ago might be said to culminate in such works as the Sydney Harbor Bridge. Truss bridges (bridges using a framework of supports) were identified as early as 55 B.C.E. Even as technology has advanced, the basic forms of bridges may be said to have changed little.

To some degree, then, the allure of the bridge, beyond its metaphorical and utilitarian aspects, may be attributed to its inherent link with the past—and its presumed link to the future. A bridge has both a name and a history that connect it to other people and places. A bridge is part of the landscape. And bridges become part of our cultural awareness. It is impossible to think of New Jersey and New York without the George Washington Bridge, or San Francisco without the Golden Gate Bridge. In his book *Engineers of Dreams*, the engineer and historian of technology Henry Petroski describes bridges as the "symbols and souls" of their cities.

In considering New Jersey's bridges, we need to explore their meanings not only in terms of history and engineering. As I have noted, bridges attract us also by their beauty. We should understand something of this aspect in order to appreciate them further.

THE BRIDGE AS ART

Since at least the Middle Ages, artists have placed bridges prominently in their depictions of landscapes and urban scenes and have even deemed them worthy of central focus. The stone arch bridge in the lower left third of El Greco's *View of Toledo* (ca. 1600) is an essential part of that landscape. In the 1880s Vincent Van Gogh made a movable bridge (drawbridge) the subject of various of his paintings at Arles. The Fauvist painter André Derain, in his 1906 *Pool of London*, put an abstraction of London's Tower Bridge in the background. Edvard Munch's iconic *The Scream* (1893) is placed on a bridge. Claude Monet's *Westminster Bridge* (1871) and Frank Stella's *Brooklyn Bridge* (1937) are two widely known modern examples.

Earlier, I used the phrase "structural art." This notion is the subject of *The Tower and the Bridge*, a book by David Billington of Princeton University about the bridge as a separate art form as well as an engineering structure. Noting that the grace and strength of bridges have inspired other forms of art, an interviewer once asked Billington about Hart Crane's poem "The Bridge" (1930). He responded that "the very fact that you can't write about a bridge without invoking a poet says something about both of 'em that is so deeply cultural that it means that the goal for the future or the image or the vision of the future is just that kind of connection."

Almost a century earlier, in a poem also titled "The Bridge," Henry Wadsworth Longfellow captured the almost confessional nature of standing on a bridge, contemplating the dark water below:

> Yet whenever I cross the river
> On its bridge with wooden piers,
> Like the odor of brine from the ocean
> Comes the thought of other years.

The bridges featured in this book have been selected not merely as documentary representations of bridge types but also as outstanding examples of bridge aesthetics. To the extent that a bridge is the embodiment of engineering principles, it is a tangible, three-dimensional expression of mathematical concepts, a sculpture of line and form. Can a bridge be deemed a work of art? Billington argued yes. Engineers continue to insist upon aesthetic considerations as a fundamental part of bridge design, and critics write about the importance of aesthetics in bridge construction. Today's engineering curricula and bridge design publications stress the need for aesthetic considerations. These concerns make sense politically as well as aesthetically. No one wants to pay taxes for an ugly bridge.

On a certain level, bridges are functional sculptures, and their grace and appeal to the senses is at least as important as their ability to withstand the forces of nature that otherwise work to destroy them. In designing the Brooklyn Bridge (1883), John Roebling declared that it "will be beautiful." Othmar H. Ammann, the extraordinarily gifted engineer who designed the George Washington Bridge (1931) and the Bayonne Steel Arch Bridge (1931) (both featured in this book), echoed Roebling:

> Economics and utility are not the engineer's only concerns. He must temper his practicality with aesthetic sensitivity. His structures should please the eye. In fact, an engineer designing a bridge is justified in making a more expensive design for beauty's sake alone. After all, many people will have to look at the bridge for the rest of their lives. Few of us appreciate eyesores, even if we should save a little money by building them.

Ammann was almost obsessive in his effort to make the George Washington Bridge as much a cultural symbol of his time as Roebling had made the Brooklyn

Bridge in his. As he and engineers before and since have recognized, bridges are meant to last, like sculptures; beyond simply facilitating transportation, they are expressions of cultural achievement of their times—or should be.

Bridges, particularly the larger ones, become indispensable features of the landscape. As an example, consider the view of the Great Beds Lighthouse (built 1880) in the Raritan River with the Outerbridge Crossing (1928) in the background (color plate 10). Here the engineering fits nicely into the environment, complementing the vista. Although it may be fashionable to decry any human construction as a scar upon the land, we must also recognize that humans are as much a part of the environment as any other animal. Why should our achievements not become part of the terrain, provided they are not destructive?

In *Aesthetics in Transportation* the U.S. Department of Transportation emphasizes that integration of engineering projects into the environment is necessary for maintenance of good order. Bridge aesthetics take into account the landscape and seek to harmonize horizontal and vertical lines with the comparable contours of the environment. Indeed, there are abandoned bridges that no longer serve a utilitarian purpose and yet are maintained because of their historic and aesthetic appeal. As Elizabeth Mock, former curator of the Museum of Modern Art's Department of Architecture, observed in her seminal *Architecture of Bridges*, "a beautiful bridge has a life quite beyond its purely practical functions."

What is "beauty"? What is a work of art? Can a scientist or an engineer be considered an artist? Such questions, debated over the centuries by artists and philosophers, certainly will not be resolved here. Most modern observers would agree, however, that bridges represent a confluence of art and technology. In *The Tower and the Bridge*, for example, Billington refers to Swiss engineer Robert Maillart (1872–1940) as an artist "who always conjures up something new through the means of expression of his time and by making use of all the possibilities at his disposal." Amid the numerous ways to solve an engineering problem, appearance—both intrinsic to the bridge and extrinsic to the bridge within its surroundings—remains an important consideration.

When the bridge itself is considered as art, it is not because of decorative add-ons. Eric Sloane, in his *American Barns and Covered Bridges*, notes that just prior to the advent of covered bridges in the United States, there was an interest in building architectural features into bridges, and often church architects were called upon for assistance. Sloane points to Lewis Wernwag, an early American bridge builder who desired to "put beauty back into the barnlike structures that Americans are throwing across their rivers."

The sixteenth-century Italian architect Andrea Palladio anticipated these concepts of aesthetics in his *Four Books on Architecture*, which appeared in 1571. In the Third Book, Palladio writes that a bridge, in essence, is a "street above water":

> [It] ought to have the same qualities that we have said were required in all other fabricks, that is, to be commodious, beautiful, and for a long time durable. They will be commodious when they are not raised above the rest of the way, and if they be raised, to have their ascent easy; and such place is to be chosen to build them in, as ought to be most convenient to the whole province, or to the whole city, according as they are to be built, either within or without the walls. . . . The place therefore to be chosen for building bridges, ought to be in the middle of the country or of the city, and as convenient to all the inhabitants as possible, and where the river has a direct course, and its bed equal, perpetual, and shallow.

Later in the same book, Palladio commended study of the bridge over the Cismone River, which divided Italy and Germany, citing that bridge for its beauty, among other reasons. Bridges constructed like this one, he wrote, are "beautiful, because the texture of the timbers is very agreeable and commodious, being even and in the same line with the remaining part of the street." In developing his ideas, Palladio relied on the Roman architect Vitruvius, whose *De Architectura*, written in the first century B.C.E., set forth the principles of *utilitas* (utility), *firmitas* (stability), and *venustas* (grace and beauty).

Early in the twentieth century Charles S. Whitney, later an engineering partner of Ammann's, made a similar point:

> Beauty is a thing apart from human progress. The old bridges themselves still form the most valuable treatise on the art of bridge design. They were built with a simplicity and sincerity which it is difficult to duplicate in this sophisticated age. These worthy veterans reflect the glory of empires, and their story is as dramatic as the political history with which it is so closely connected.

That such artistic considerations continue to engage engineers into the twenty-first century is evidenced by recent literature on the subject. In his *Bridgescape* (1998), the American engineer Frederick Gottemoeller provided guidelines for aesthetic considerations in bridge design. The late, renowned German engineer Fritz Leonhardt, in his *Bridges: Aesthetics and Design* (1984), discussed the aesthetics of bridges in light of philosophical considerations of beauty and explored the manner in which people react to geometric lines and the cultural role of proportions. The real issue, he argued, is how people perceive and process the aesthetic messages from objects, and how those perceptions relate to bridge design. In seeking to determine what characteristics or guidelines engineers should employ, he identified purpose, proportion, order, form, integration into the environment, surface texture, color, character, complexity and variety, and incorporation of Nature. He also emphasized the need for ethics in aesthetics; that is, as we place artificial structures in the environment, we have an ethical obligation to make them beautiful.

Paul Gauvreau of the University of Toronto has reviewed what he calls the "conventional wisdom on bridge aesthetics" and argues that "if bridge design is to be recognized as a valid and distinct means of artistic expression, then bridges must reflect the truths that define the fundamental essence shared by all works of art, regardless of the medium of expression." Gauvreau's major point is that a bridge's structural efficiency is not sufficient alone to confer artistic merit. He also draws a distinction between engineering vision and architectural vision, disputing that only the latter can approach art. In other words, those engineers who seek to make their bridges works of art must look to other sources. In certain cases, such as the Benjamin Franklin and George Washington bridges, architects were involved. Gauvreau does not seem to deny that engineers are capable of creating art in their bridges. Rather, he seems to suggest that one cannot take a simple mathematical construct, embodied in a bridge, and automatically call it art. Even David Billington does not contend that every bridge is automatically "art." There must be some identifiable standards by which to judge.

The bridges of New Jersey featured here are, I suggest, examples of structural art. There is an elegance to the Pulaski Skyway (1932), recognized at the time, which can be discerned amidst the roughness of the region it crosses. The George Washington Bridge's structural simplicity—particularly its transparent towers—and starkness of form resonate with the viewer. As Elizabeth Mock has stated eloquently:

> Since the reality of a bridge lies in its structure, the art of bridge building lies in the recognition and development of the beauty latent in those structural forms that most effectively exploit the strength and special properties of a given material. Beauty is not automatic; technical perfection alone is not enough. A great engineer is not a slave to his formulas. He is an artist who uses his calculations as tools to create working shapes as inevitable and harmonious in their appearance as the natural laws behind them. He handles his material with poetic insight, revealing its inmost nature while extracting its ultimate strength through structure appropriate to its unique powers.

No one was more blunt than Amman, who once stated that "it is a crime to build an ugly bridge."

These observations provide a context for viewing the bridges of New Jersey as structural art.

BRIDGE TYPES

Apart from appreciating the aesthetics of bridges, we need to understand something about their engineering. Bridges are categorized according to their structural characteristics, with the problem of the particular crossing often dictating the type of bridge to be built. Some crossings may permit consideration of alternative proposals as to type and within type; different materials may be used for bridges of the same type; and engineers may even combine two or more different types as sections of a single bridge.

Various writers offer different categories for the types of bridges. Some refer to three types: beam, arch, and suspension. Others break down the suspension bridge into traditional suspension and cable-stayed bridges. Still others subsume the cantilever within the beam bridge, which itself is sometimes referred to as a "stringer" bridge. Taking into consideration all of these differences, I find useful seven categories for the purpose of identifying the general types of bridges featured in this book: arch, truss, covered, cantilever, suspension, movable, and girder. No attempt has been made to seek examples of every subtype or variation. For example, the cable-stayed bridge, a type of suspension bridge that is becoming more common domestically as well as internationally, is not found in New Jersey. (The nearest examples include the Chesapeake and Delaware Canal Bridge in Delaware and the Charles River Bridge in Boston.) Likewise, as mentioned, a single bridge may adapt features from different types, and many bridges will involve truss configurations of one kind or another. Within the specified categories, however, New Jersey boasts the largest highway cantilever bridge in the United States (Commodore John Barry Bridge), some of the leading suspension bridges (George Washington and Benjamin Franklin bridges), one of the three largest steel arch bridges (Bayonne Bridge), and numerous notable and historic truss bridges.

For a better understanding of these types, certain basic engineering issues need to be explained. First, the type of bridge chosen for a particular situation depends upon its ability to resolve the issues of force, among them, the pressures of load, distance and elevation, and velocity of wind. The bridge must also satisfy non-natural forces, namely, political and economic considerations. The bridge has to be financed; people and businesses may be dislocated; military interests will insist that navigable waters remaining passable. Environmental and aesthetic issues must also be addressed. From an aesthetic standpoint, few bridge types can rival a multi-arch span across a river between mountains; but if high clearance is needed to allow ships to pass, a cantilever, suspension, or movable bridge may be more appropriate.

As a start, we can turn again to Squire Whipple's famous "Essay on Bridge Building" to frame the problem that a bridge must solve in order to sustain itself against the forces of nature and remain consistent with the laws of physics:

> Here, then, we have the elementary idea, the grand fundamental principal [*sic*] in bridge-building. Whatever form of structure be adopted, the elementary object to be accomplished is, to sustain a given weight in a given position, by a system of oblique forces whose resultant shall pass through the center of gravity of the body, in a vertically upward direction, in circumstances where the weight cannot be conveniently met by a simple force in the same line, and opposite to, that of gravity.

Whipple expressed succinctly what contemporary engineers understand. That is, bridges must carry various weights, including their own, called the "dead load." They must also support the "live loads" that pass over them—the vehicular, pedestrian, or rail traffic, or combinations of these. Finally, bridges must support "environmental loads," such as the impact of rain or wind.

Engineers speak of compression and tension. Compression is the force that presses materials together or shortens them, whereas tension is the force that tries to pull materials apart or stretches them. The same structure can have both forces acting upon it simultaneously. For example, a deck (the roadway or railway over which traffic passes) supported only at the two ends will have a tendency to sag both from its own weight and from weight placed upon it. The top portion of the deck is in compression as the downward force of gravity seeks to push its elements together, and the bottom portion is in tension as its members try to spread out. (Imagine a straight line turning into the letter "u": the top portion is being squeezed together while the bottom portion is splaying outward.) Mastery of compression and tension depends upon the support provided as well as the materials used. Variations on these forces involve sideways motion: "shear" occurs when parts of the structure cut across each other; "torsion" refers to the twisting of one part while another holds firm or twists in the opposite direction, straining the parts.

A span is the distance between two supports. A single-span *beam bridge* consists simply of a deck laid across two supports. The forces of compression and tension are in balance, and the beam remains rigid, provided it is thick enough and the supports strong enough. Because the forces act directly on the deck, materials that have sufficient tensile strength, such as steel, are used in its construction. Stone is not suitable for a beam bridge because its strength lies in compression, not tension; rather than sag, the deck would break if the pulling force was too great. The longer the beam, the thicker or stronger the material must be. A beam bridge may involve multiple spans of deck beams carried over multiple supports; these are "continuous beam" bridges. In some instances the beams may be slightly curved; although the bridge resembles an arch bridge, it does not really involve the principles of arching action.

A variation on the beam bridge is the *girder bridge*, which allows spanning of greater distances because of the properties of the girder. Box girder bridges, first invented in the 1840s by the Englishman Robert Stephenson, became popular in the United States in the twentieth century. The beam is a deep hollow box that has either a rectangular or a trapezoidal cross section. The Bow Bridge in New York City's Central Park is said to be the oldest extant wrought-iron girder bridge in the United States. Several of New Jersey's girder bridges are pictured in this book (see the Edison Bridge, featured in color plate 15).

A *cantilever bridge* is another variation on the beam bridge. The easiest way to envision a cantilever bridge is to imagine two diving boards aimed at each other. Instead of a single deck beam supported at each end by a pier, two beams are each balanced on a pier, with the longer ends facing each other and the shorter ends anchored to counterbalance the weight. An additional center span may be placed between them and supported by them. As with a simple beam, the live and dead loads balance each other.

An *arch bridge* has a parabolic shape, and allows the live and dead loads to act in unison in compression, forcing the materials together and thus maintaining the structural integrity of the bridge. In an arch bridge, the compressive forces are directed outward along the path of the arch and carried to the ground, so that the deck does not have to bear the direct downward pressure itself. The need for material that can withstand compression made stone a natural choice for arch bridges from earliest times. Steel, which has both compressive and tensile strength, was later used for arch bridges and enabled the design and use of longer spans. Among the different types of arch bridges are the *fixed arch*, which is shallowest at the center and becomes deeper toward the supports (also known as abutments), and the *hinged arch*, which has a flexible joint where each end of the arch meets its support. (The "hinge" is a pin connection joining the arch components; a hinged arch bridge should not be confused with a drawbridge.) A masonry arch bridge is a concrete bridge in the shape of an arch. The limestone Anji Bridge in China, completed in the early seventh century, is the oldest surviving arch bridge in China and the oldest segmented arch bridge in the world. It employs a more flattened arch (instead of a half-circle shape), trading greater stress on the supports for a longer span.

The *suspension bridge* is generally composed of four main elements: a deck over which traffic passes, towers, cables, and anchors. As the name indicates, the deck is suspended by cables. In the simplest form, the ropes or cables are strung across supporting towers and fastened securely in anchors at each end. The anchorage blocks are generally made of steel and reinforced concrete. The vertical lines strung from the cables and holding the deck are in tension; it is the ground beneath the towers that is in compression, being pushed down. A variation is the *cable-stayed bridge*, in which the cables that suspend the deck are anchored to the tower alone. Various authors debate the early origins of the cable-stayed bridge. Although the concept may be traced back to Faustus Verantius's *Machinae Novae* (New Machine, 1595), the failure of the Dryburgh Abbey Bridge in Scotland in 1818 seems to have caused the disuse of the form for some time. Today, most sources credit the German engineer Fritz Leonhardt with developing the modern form of this type of suspension bridge.

Trusses are braced frames, generally composed of triangular panels, that provide additional support to various types of bridges. The triangle, geometrically and physically, is a rigid form and the only shape that does not collapse when pressure is applied to one side. As early as the sixteenth century, Palladio described the use of the truss as a stabilizing feature. Trusses helped support timber bridges and gave the wooden deck additional support that allowed for spans of greater distances and stability. They have also been used to support the decks on suspension bridges and in conjunction with cantilever bridges. Covered bridges are enclosed truss bridges, and trusses can add support to an arch bridge. Sometimes a renovated truss bridge will have the truss superstructure intact, but the structure itself may be essentially a beam bridge, with the truss actually offering no structural support and remaining more for decoration. A truss bridge should not be confused with a simple beam bridge because the method of support for the deck is different.

Movable bridges are capable of shifting position in whole or in part. Essentially, they have a mechanism whereby the bridge rotates, or parts of it lift, to allow traffic to pass on either side or beneath. These bridges may be considered to be beam bridges, although not uncommonly, like the Tacony-Palmyra, they combine other features, such as arches and trusses.

BRIDGE MATERIALS

The need to balance the impact of natural forces may be met by a variety of materials, but not all materials will serve in all circumstances. For example, there may be a preference for one material, but cost may rule it out. The five basic materials historically used for bridge construction are wood, stone, iron, concrete, and steel (including steel used to make reinforced and prestressed concrete). At present, bridges are generally constructed of steel, reinforced concrete, or prestressed concrete, or a combination of these materials.

Stone and wood were the earliest and most obvious choices for bridge construction because of their availability. Most Roman bridges, for example, were made of wood. As noted earlier, the compressive qualities of stone made it a natural choice for arch bridges. The Roman stone arch was a semicircle and made use of *voussoirs*, wedge-shaped stones cut to fit together. The evenly placed voussoirs formed an "arch ring" that was crowned in the middle by a "keystone" held in place by its own weight and the force of gravity. Another type of arch, the *corbel*, is more like a cantilever. The stones are laid on top of each other, with each succeeding edge protruding beyond the edge of the one below.

Iron as a material became available in large quantities around 1750, but its major use in bridge construction occurred from 1850 through 1890. With the growth of rail transportation, iron bridges were considered more suitable than masonry arch bridges to handle the stress of a moving train over short crossings. Two types of iron were used. The first, cast iron, is an iron alloy with approximately 2.0 to 4.5 percent carbon; as its name suggests, it is poured into molds. Wrought (worked) iron is a softer, more malleable metal, with approximately 0.1 to 0.2 percent carbon or less. Cast iron was stronger in tensile strength than masonry, and it also had stronger compressive properties. Wrought iron had tensile as well as compressive qualities and was considered the better bridge-building material. Although more brittle, cast iron was cheaper and easier to produce, and it became the material of choice for bridges built during the Industrial Revolution.

The first proposal to construct an iron bridge seems to have come from Robert Mylne in England in 1774. His design for an iron arch bridge for Inverary, Strathclyde, in Scotland, was never built. Contemporaneously, Thomas Pritchard was working on designs for three types of bridges: a timber-trussed arch bridge; a masonry bridge on a cast-iron center; and a cast-iron bridge between brick abutments. Pritchard's latter design ultimately took form as the first cast-iron bridge, known as the Iron Bridge, built between 1777 and 1779 at Coalbrookdale in Shropshire, England. Here we should also take note of an American's contribution: Thomas Paine, more widely known as a political activist and author of *Common Sense*, obtained a patent in 1788 for an iron bridge with five cast-iron ribs.

Concrete is generally made from water, sand, stone, and a binding element, such as cement. The use of concrete predates the Romans, but they developed their own version around 300 B.C.E., using lime and pozzolana from the Pozzouli area near the Bay of Naples. After the Roman Empire fell around 400 C.E., the use of concrete for bridge construction fell into abeyance until the Industrial Revolution. In the 1750s the British engineer John Smeaton experimented with new types of cement as the binding agent. Portland cement, invented and patented in 1824 by Joseph Aspdin, became the basis for concrete foundations. (Its name derived from its resemblance to stone quarried on the Isle of Portland.) The first Portland cement plant in the United States was established in 1871 in Coplay, Pennsylvania, and in 1916 the Portland Cement Association was founded.

As steel and iron became cheaper to produce, their value in combination with concrete became evident. Concrete by itself is weak in tensile strength. Reinforced concrete has iron or steel rods embedded in the material to combine the metal's tensile advantages with concrete's compressive strength. The concrete protects the enclosed metal from corrosion, while the steel lessens the amount of concrete needed. In 1867 a French gardener, Joseph Monier, patented his system of embedding iron-wire mesh in concrete tubs and basins to strengthen them. He and others soon recognized the implications for larger structures. The German engineer G. A. Wayss purchased the rights to Monier's patent in 1879 and pioneered reinforced concrete construction in Austria and Germany in the 1880s. In the United States, in 1884, Ernest L. Ransome patented a reinforcing system using twisted rods. Ransome built the first reinforced concrete bridge in the United States, the Lake Alvord Bridge, in San Francisco in 1889.

Billington notes in *Robert Maillart's Bridges* that "[t]he use of reinforced concrete became widespread only after 1894." Citing a 1904 study by the American Society of Civil Engineers, he contends that "no important concrete-steel bridge had been built in the United States" before 1894. Later in the twentieth century, however, some large American bridges used reinforced concrete.

The Swiss engineer Robert Maillart (1872–1940) recognized the aesthetic properties of reinforced concrete. In discussing Maillart's masterpiece, the Salginatobel Bridge (1930), David Billington explains, "Maillart created in the wilderness a bridge of such extraordinary beauty that its material, reinforced concrete, became the medium for a legitimate style in its own right." In Billington's estimation, "Maillart was the first engineer to sense that the full expression in concrete structures could be efficient (safe performance with minimum materials), economical (accountable to the public welfare or private industry with competitive costs), and elegant all in the same construction."

Another bridge material, prestressed concrete, locks in tensile properties before placement by embedding stretched steel strands, which has the effect of neutralizing the tensile forces that later affect the bridge. Holes for the steel tendons are curved so that the tendons, once fitted, anchor at each end and pull the concrete beam together into compression. One advantage of prestressed concrete is that less steel and concrete need to be used, allowing for less expensive and lighter structures, even elegant ones. Some historians of technology credit French engineer Eugène Freyssinet (1879–1962) with the development of prestressed concrete in 1927, to remedy the downward "creep" he observed in the three-arch Le Veurdre Bridge (1910). The Saale Bridge (1927), an arch bridge in Alsleben, Germany, designed by Franz Dischinger (1887–1953), is said to be the first prestressed concrete bridge. In the 1950s another German engineer, Ulrich Finsterwalder (1897–1988), developed a system for building concrete cantilever bridges in segments. In the United States, the first significant prestressed concrete bridge was the Walnut Lane Bridge (1950), a girder bridge in Philadelphia.

Toward the end of the nineteenth century, bridges built of steel came into their own. Steel, which is basically wrought iron with chromium, nickel, manganese, and comparable metals substituting for proportionate amounts of carbon, combined the advantages of cast and wrought iron without the disadvantages of those materials. As a replacement for stone, steel allowed for ever longer arch bridges. In the context of suspension bridges, steel cables replaced chains.

The substitutions were not without incident. In 1879, for example, the railroad bridge at the Firth of Tay in Scotland collapsed. The successor bridge at the Firth of Forth was built of steel, but designed with cantilever principles to withstand the environmental forces. In the United States, the Queensboro Bridge in New York City, designed by Gustav Lindenthal, did not have suspended sections, as did the Forth Bridge, and was made of nickel steel. Nor was stone completely abandoned. The Brooklyn Bridge had stone towers, although they were intended as much for aesthetic as for engineering purposes. The George Washington Bridge was origi-nally supposed to have stone encasing the steel tower framework, but that design was abandoned for cost reasons.

Steel suspension bridges were favored in the first half of the twentieth century. Among these, the George Washington, Benjamin Franklin, and Golden Gate bridges have achieved world renown.

THE ENGINEERS

It is, perhaps, a sign of great art or engineering when a work speaks for itself. Nevertheless, behind every great bridge there can be found a personality and a story.

In 1811 Thomas Pope complained, "It is a notorious fact that there is no country in the world which is more in need of good and permanent Bridges than the United States of America." He nevertheless acknowledged that "[n]ecessity has already produced some handsome and extensive specimens of bridge-building in the United States." Arch and truss bridges marked these early efforts, and inventors often patented their various designs for trusses. William Howe's original truss, for example, was built of timber strengthened by cast-iron vertical king-post tension members. The Pratt truss, on the other hand, put the tensile forces on cast-iron diagonals, with wooden king posts. Squire Whipple, author of *A Work on Bridge-Building* (1847), used a bowstring configuration that combined the use of cast iron and wrought iron in different ties. This diversity reflects the unique perspective and thinking of individual engineers.

Several of the key figures in the history of American engineering, and of bridge building in particular, had direct or indirect connections to the bridges of New Jersey. As background for later discussions, brief summaries of the careers of some of the more prominent individuals are featured here in chronological order, along with a quick look at some of the companies that built their bridges. New Jer-sey is distinguished not only for its remarkable heritage of internationally renowned bridges, but also for the important contributions to bridge engineering that took place within its borders.

JOHN ROEBLING

One of the preeminent engineers of the nineteenth century, John Augustus Roeb-ling (1806–1869) was born in Thuringia, Germany, and studied engineering, bridge construction, and philosophy at the Royal Polytechnic Institute in Berlin. After graduation, he built roads in Germany and then emigrated to the United States in 1831 with his brother Karl to establish an agrarian community in Pennsylvania called Saxonburg, which failed. He became an American citizen in 1837 and began working on canal projects for the state of Pennsylvania. His suspension aqueducts earned him a national reputation; one still stands at Lackawaxen, Pennsylvania, over the Delaware River. In 1841 Roebling established a factory to produce wire rope to replace the hemp rope cables used on canal boats. These cables were used in his suspension bridges, the first of which was built in 1846–1847 across the Monongahela River in Pittsburgh. In the late 1840s he relocated his wire rope factory to Trenton and soon afterward supervised construction of the 810-foot Niagara Gorge railroad suspension bridge (1851–1855).

Roebling's most famous project was the Brooklyn Bridge, engineered with his son Washington. While he was on a survey pontoon attempting to fix a tower location, his foot was crushed and subsequently amputated. He died of tetanus a few weeks later. The historic town of Roebling, built for company workers near Florence, New Jersey, still stands. A memorial statue erected in John Roebling's honor is in Cadwalader Park, Trenton.

JOHN ALEXANDER LOW WADDELL

J.A.L. Waddell (1854–1938), a Canadian-born engineer, founded two engineering firms that survive to this day. Waddell graduated from Rensselaer Polytechnic Institute in 1875 with a degree in civil engineering, and also received degrees from McGill University in Montreal. He worked around the world on various engineering projects, including railroads. In addition to teaching rational and technical mechanics at Rensselaer, he taught civil engineering at the Imperial University of Japan in Tokyo (1882–1886).

In 1886 or 1887 Waddell opened a practice as a consulting engineer in Kansas City, Missouri. He left for New York in 1920 and later, with his protégé from Kansas City days, Shortridge Hardesty, formed Waddell and Hardesty, which specialized in vertical lift bridges. They later expanded their practice to include highway bridges. Waddell wrote several works on bridge construction, including *De Pontibus* (1898), and held a patent for the Waddell "A" Truss Bridge, derived from the king-post truss. Donald Jackson, in *Great American Bridges and Dams*, describes Waddell's efforts "to find a way of building a rigid, short-span, pin-connected truss that could economically carry heavy, fast-moving railroad traffic without excessive deflection or vibration." His bridge designs were used extensively in the 1890s in the Midwest and Japan, according to Jackson. U.S. Patent Office records show that Waddell held patents (with others) for vertical lift bridges, truss bridges, bascule bridges (draw-bridges), and suspension bridges, or improvements to them. In New Jersey, J.A.L. Waddell Consulting Engineers was responsible for the Lower Hackensack Draw-bridge (railroad bridge) in Jersey City, across the Hackensack River.

A brief discussion of Waddell's career must at least mention the bitter rivalry between him and Gustav Lindenthal (discussed at length by Petroski in *Engineers of Dreams*). Both men influenced some of the country's most important engineers and engineering firms. In his 1916 book *Bridge Engineering*, Waddell criticized Lindenthal's design of the Queensboro (Blackwell's Island) Bridge. Lindenthal, in turn, excoriated his rival in a review of that book. He claimed that Waddell's

> repeated references to aesthetic appearances based on nothing more than curves in the top or bottom chords will appear to others as rather naïve. . . . For any bridge structure requiring architectural consideration the bridge engineer will do well to consult a competent architect; and experience has shown that not every architect is competent here.

Their dispute offers another perspective on the place of aesthetics in bridge building and also highlights the controversy over the roles of architect and engineer in bridge design.

RALPH MODJESKI

Among the bridges designed by Ralph Modjeski (1861–1940) are the Tacony-Palmyra and the Benjamin Franklin in New Jersey and the Quebec Bridge in Canada. Born in Poland (his original name was Rudolphe Modrzejewski), he first visited the United States with his mother, a well-known actress, in 1876. By 1878, he had chosen engineering over a career as a concert pianist. He studied at Ecole des Pontes et Chaussées in Paris, received his engineering degree in 1885, returned to the United States, and began work with George S. Morison, a noted bridge engineer. Modjeski struck out on his own in 1893 in Chicago, and in 1923 joined Frank M. Masters to establish the firm Modjeski and Masters, which continues to this day. Other bridges designed by the firm include the Ambassador Bridge across the Detroit River between Detroit and Sandwich, Ontario; the Mid-Hudson Bridge across the Hudson River at Poughkeepsie, New York; and the San Francisco–Oakland Bay Bridge. In *Engineers of Dreams*, Petroski mentions that Modjeski was once described by Ralph Budd, president of the Great Northern Railway, as an artist who chose "to express himself [in] steel and stone and concrete." Such an appreciation recalls Billington's assessment of Maillart.

JOSEPH BAERMANN STRAUSS

Born in Cincinnati, Joseph Baermann (J. B.) Strauss (1870–1938) shared a German ancestry with Roebling and Othmar Ammann. A brief teaching career followed his graduation from the University of Cincinnati in 1892. Strauss then worked as principal assistant engineer for Ralph Modjeski in Chicago from 1899 until he left for private practice in 1902 and formed Strauss Engineering in 1904. The corporation, with offices in Chicago and San Francisco, specialized in movable and long-span bridges.

Strauss's success with suspension bridges might be said to have culminated with his design for the Golden Gate Bridge, but that was only one area of his expertise. He developed various types of bascule bridges and was largely responsible for their increased popularity. He also invented portable searchlight outfits used in World War I, and his work on a "yielding barrier" to stop automobiles at railroad crossings evolved into the system adopted by the navy for stopping planes on aircraft carrier decks. Perhaps more of a Renaissance man than others of the engineers featured here, Strauss founded the American Citizenship Foundation and contributed to literary and poetic magazines and journals. One wonders where he found the time to write the paradoxically titled *By-Products of Idle Hours* (1921).

OTHMAR AMMANN

Othmar Ammann (1879–1965) was one of the twentieth century's greatest bridge builders. He came to the United States in 1904, after graduating from the Swiss Federal Institute of Technology in Zurich. His first job, with Joseph Mayer, a consulting engineer whose firm specialized in designing long-span steel bridges, provided Ammann with relevant experience. While with Mayer, he worked on at least thirty steel bridges, and was exposed to various designs and proposals for Hudson River crossings.

A slowdown in work at the Mayer firm led Ammann to join the engineering staff of the Pennsylvania Steel Company. During one of several breaks in his career at Pennsylvania Steel, Ammann was hired by renowned engineer Ralph Modjeski in Chicago, where he worked on steel bridges for the Oregon Trunk Railroad. Rejoining Pennsylvania Steel, Ammann supervised a design team and became acquainted with another important engineer, Frederic C. Kunz. Kunz persuaded Ammann to leave Pennsylvania Steel and join him in Philadelphia in 1909. This move, as Darl Rastorfer notes in *Six Bridges*, "continued to advance Ammann along a career path that focused on long-span steel structures . . . a specialty that supported relatively few practitioners." He contributed to the significant work *Design of Steel Bridges* (1915) by Kunz and their other partner, Charles C. Schneider.

Ammann wanted to return to Europe, but another prominent engineer, Gustav Lindenthal, persuaded him to stay. In 1912 Ammann began work with Lindenthal on the famed Hell Gate Bridge in New York. Rastorfer calls it "a stunning landmark to the Industrial Age's boundless vision and unshakable self-confidence," a structure that "bristles with strength and energy." Ammann apparently maintained an uneasy on-again/off-again relationship with Lindenthal and his firm, departing several times to return to Switzerland and once to work for the Just Such Clay Company in Perth Amboy, New Jersey. From 1925 through 1939 he was director of engineering for the Port Authority of New York and New Jersey, entering private practice in 1939. Seven years later he formed the engineering firm of Ammann and Whitney with Charles S. Whitney, an engineer from Milwaukee, Wisconsin.

Ammann was chief engineer or otherwise assisted on many important New Jersey bridges, including the Goethals, Outerbridge Crossing, Walt Whitman, Delaware Memorial, Bayonne, and George Washington. His rivalry with engineer David Steinman is noted in the discussion of the George Washington Bridge. Ammann also served on the board of engineers overseeing the Golden Gate Bridge construction.

In an interview for Public Broadcasting's "Great Projects" series, Gay Talese, author of *The Bridge* (about the Verrazano-Narrows Bridge), reflected on Ammann as an artist:

> My assumption about Mr. Ammann—I met him a few times as you know, but did not ever get to know him—my assumption is that he was a, a very private person who expressed himself as an artist on this grand scale that is characteristic of builders of bridges. He was a great designer whose concept was outlined against the sky. He found in New York . . . the perfect setting for his artistic expression where his works could span masses of land but be written across the sky in steel and cables. And so he was in the great tradition of all great art, a large thinking man with more of a sense of what he was doing than in a sense of who he, himself, was.

MORRIS GOODKIND

Morris Goodkind (1888–1968) was chief bridge engineer with the New Jersey Highway Department from 1925 through 1955. Graduating from Columbia University with a degree in civil engineering in 1910, he first worked in New York for Albert Lucius, whose commissions included elevated railroad systems. In addition to private practice, Goodkind's career included stints with the New York Interboro

Rapid Transit Corporation, the New Jersey Highway Department, and Mercer County, New Jersey (as county engineer). He received the prestigious Phoebe Hobson Fowler Medal from the American Society of Civil Engineers for the bridge now named for him, the Morris Goodkind Bridge, which spans the Raritan River near New Brunswick. Although Goodkind may not have the national name recognition of the other engineers discussed here, his influence on New Jersey bridges was significant. He was particularly concerned with bridge aesthetics.

THE BRIDGE COMPANIES

A brief note is in order about the companies that actually built the bridges. In the great age of bridge construction, from perhaps the mid-nineteenth century through the first quarter of the twentieth century, numerous bridge-building companies operated throughout the United States. It was not uncommon for established companies to spawn new ones as employees left to form their own firms. In New Jersey, approximately nineteen companies are listed in the Directory of American Bridge Building Companies for the period 1840–1900. Among the more notable was the Passaic Rolling Mill Company (1877–1901) in Paterson, which in 1884 had a fabricating capacity of 12,000 tons a year—"one of the largest of that time," according to the directory. In Trenton, apart from John A. Roebling's Sons Company, there was another famous bridge company: the New Jersey Steel and Iron Company (1866–1900), which was acquired by the American Bridge Company, based in Chicago.

At the turn of the twentieth century, the American Bridge Company was among the largest bridge-building firms in America, according to the directory. Begun in 1870 by Lucius B. Boomer, its early principals included the brother-in-law of William Howe, inventor of the Howe truss. The company's name changed with subsequent owners. It was liquidated in 1878 as the result of the general economic climate, problematic contracts, and failures associated with its involvement with the Poughkeepsie Bridge Company's railroad bridge project. Reappearing in 1891 as a new company called the American Bridge Works, it bought back its plant and five years later, in 1900, was acquired by J. P. Morgan's New York–based American Bridge Company, which was incorporated in New Jersey on April 14, 1900. Before it was acquired in 1901 by U.S. Steel, the American Bridge Company bought twenty-four companies (including the Berlin Iron Bridge Company, the King Bridge Company, and the Wrought Iron Bridge Company, all of which are represented by at least one of the bridges in this book) and controlled fully half of

American fabricating capability. (The present American Bridge Company Web site refers to twenty-seven merged companies in 1900, with 90 percent of all American bridge-building works.) In 1987 the company was cut loose from U.S. Steel (by then USX Corporation) and has been privately owned since, with its headquarters in Pittsburgh.

THE LAW AND POLITICS OF BRIDGES

It is beyond the scope of this work to engage in a lengthy or technical discussion of the federal and state laws, including both statute and regulation, that govern bridges. Generally speaking, congressional authorization is necessary for construction of bridges involving interstate and navigable waterways, although it remains to individual states to enact appropriate implementing legislation.

Federal law regulates the construction of bridges over navigable waters and, to ensure safe passage of marine traffic, requires that the secretary of defense must approve the plans. Certain regional entities, such as the Port Authority of New York and New Jersey and the Delaware River Port Authority, have legal authority over bridges that they are authorized by statute to construct and own. For example, the New Jersey and New York legislatures expressly authorized the Outerbridge Crossing and Goethals Bridge; in each case the Port Authority determined the bridge's site, size, type, and method of construction, but the municipalities through which the approaches passed maintained approval rights for highway extensions or changes.

At the state level, any bridge across the Delaware River is governed by a special group of statutes that created the Delaware River Joint Toll Bridge Commission and authorized the governor to enter into compacts or agreements on behalf of New Jersey with Pennsylvania to build bridge facilities. Formation of bridge companies is also regulated by statute. Five or more persons, a majority of whom must be residents of New Jersey, may form a company for the purpose of constructing, maintaining, and operating a bridge. Tolls may be charged. Interestingly, a separate statute concerns the formation of Delaware River bridge companies, which require only three members, who need not be New Jersey residents. These bridge companies may charge tolls. If they have not been acquired by the state within fifty years, the bridges become the property of the state at the end of that period.

One of the recurrent themes in the history of transportation in New Jersey was the conflict between ferry and bridge. As a matter of law, ferry companies were compensated for being put out of business. In 1871, in the case of *The Columbia and Delaware Bridge Company v. Geise*, 34 N.J.L. 268 (E&A 1870), the Court of Errors and Appeals held that ferry owners—or in this case, their widows and heirs—could claim damages under the statute for loss of business as a matter of common law, regardless of whether the ferry was in existence at the time of the construction of the bridge. From the perspective of the twenty-first century, the decision stands as an interesting attempt to protect an obsolete business overtaken by technology.

A FINAL WORD

This book is about more than simply the physical presence of New Jersey's bridges. It is about memorializing and elevating these structures to the level of artistic appreciation and also about recognizing their ability to connect us to each other, to our past and our future, and bringing to life the stories around them. As so many others have commented, bridges are physical representations of our culture. They are about the people who built them and treasured them, and in some cases died creating them. Gay Talese wrote in the opening lines of *The Bridge* that "a great bridge is a poetic construction of enduring beauty and utility." David McCullough similarly wrote in his story of the Brooklyn Bridge:

> There was, after all, something quite special about a bridge, almost any bridge. Very few were ever outright ugly, and when built right, with everything in harmony, with everything superfluous done away with, with all elements doing exactly what they were supposed to, then a bridge was a thrilling thing to see, with its own kind of graceful majesty, something quite apart from the practicalities of engineering.

It is with these thoughts in mind that I embarked upon this project. The bridges presented here are part of the history of this state, this country, and, to some extent, international engineering. The George Washington Bridge and the Benjamin Franklin Bridge, when built, were the longest suspension bridges in the world. The Bayonne Bridge was the longest arch bridge, and the Commodore Barry Bridge remains a world record holder for cantilever bridges. At the other end of the spectrum, stone arch bridges like the Stony Brook Bridge provide a direct link to America's Revolutionary past. They are works of art that I have sought to capture and describe, mainly through imagery but also through words.

ARCH BRIDGES

The simplest and most primitive bridge is undoubtedly a plank or tree laid across a stream, supported by the land at each end and perhaps by a series of rocks placed in the stream. However, there are problems with beam bridges. Unless they are supported regularly, their reach is limited; and unless their supports are high enough, marine or other traffic cannot pass beneath. An early solution to these issues was the arch bridge, which takes advantage of natural laws of physics to support a deck high above the crossing. Gravity holds the elements of the bridge in place as they are pressed against each other by the downward force, which is distributed along the path of the arch to the ground. This distribution allowed for larger spans without intermediate support. Consequently, the arch bridge was useful for spanning distances greater than was possible with simple beams.

Stone was an apt material for arch bridges, because it has compressive strength, meaning that it can withstand the pressure of pushing on it. There are two basic types of stone arches (and variations within those). The first, the corbel arch, is created by a series of stones or bricks laid on top of each other, with the ends extended in a kind of cantilever construction: three-quarters of the weight of each stone or brick supports the one-quarter overhang. Ultimately, like two staircases rising toward each other, the piles from opposite sides meet at the top.

The second type of stone arch, the voussoir arch (also known as the "true arch"), is based on the parabolic placement of like-sized components. To build this bridge, a temporary structure called falsework was employed, on which the stones were laid until the keystone was placed in the center so that the structure could sustain itself.

In discussions of stone arch bridges, some vocabulary is used that has particular meaning. Different sources use different definitions, and various of the sources cited in the bibliography offer their own definitions. I have sought a composite for purposes of this book. *Rubble* means irregular, uncut, rough stones or stone fragments. *Ashlar* indicates cut, square, or rectangular stone placed adjacent to other such stones. *Random* refers to stones placed in no particular order and of different shapes, either gathered from nearby or received that way from a quarry. Random placement is to be contrasted with *coursed*, in which the stones are placed in rows. A *mosaic* configuration is a pattern of different-sized stones fitted together. Thus, a "random rubble" bridge would consist of irregularly sized stones in no particular order, with smaller stones filling gaps, whereas "coursed rubble" would be different-sized stones placed in clearly discernible rows. *Gauged* stones have gone through a grinding process that reduces all of them to the same thickness. A *parapet* is a low protective wall or fence at the edge of a bridge. A *spandrel* is the flat vertical surface bounded by an arch on either side, with the tops of the arches bounding it at the top; it may be *open* (forming its own apparent arch) or *closed* (solid). The *abutment* is the support at each end of the arch. Arches may be *pointed* instead of *rounded*.

Stone, of course, is not the only material suitable for the construction of an arch bridge. By the closing decades of the nineteenth century, steel became preferable to stone for constructing arch bridges because it could span longer distances and because it had an aesthetic appeal. Whereas stone bridges required the roadway to curve with the arch, steel permitted a flat deck, where traffic could go "through" the arch, or a flat deck on top of the arch. Concrete could also be used, as it was for two of the bridges in Newark's Branch Brook Park that are featured in this section.

Although the construction of large stone arch bridges entailed significant expense, smaller ones, often built by local people, were common in New Jersey in the eighteenth and nineteenth centuries. The availability of stone and rock made it relatively easy to span short distances across creeks and small rivers without theoretical calculations to determine the support requirements. Nonetheless, care had to be taken if the bridge were to last. It was not until Squire Whipple wrote his bridge-building treatise in the first half of the nineteenth century that a meaningful effort was made to bring scientific and mathematical precision to American bridge design and construction. In the days before mathematical calculations, bridges seem to have been built by rules of thumb, or trial and error.

In his book on the bridges of North America, David Plowden identifies the earliest stone arch bridge in the United States as the Frankford Avenue Bridge over Pennypack Creek in Philadelphia, built in 1697. In New Jersey, the remnants of the oldest surviving stone arch bridge are said to be located in Bound Brook, in Somerset County. The New Jersey Historic Bridge Survey dates it to 1743 and further notes that no stone arch bridges are known south of Trenton. The largest of the stone arch bridges in colonial New Jersey, Wheaton J. Lane believed, was in Trenton over Assunpink Creek. In his study of travel and transportation in New Jersey, Lane also pointed out the high cost of stone arch bridges and their infrequency in New Jersey, and Donald C. Jackson, in *Great American Bridges and Dams*, contends that the stone arch bridge was never quite as popular in this country as it was in Europe.

Nevertheless, judging by the number of stone arch bridges still standing, particularly in New Jersey, we may conclude that many people in this state did in fact consider them worthwhile, economical, and necessary to build. In Hunterdon County alone, a bridge survey under the direction of Professor Thomas Boothby of Pennsylvania State University identified more than one hundred stone arch bridges. Boothby notes that the construction of such bridges in that county "almost exclusively arose from the response of a local agricultural community" and that they "represent a significant advancement in regional development for the bridge type reflects the progress and prosperity of the region."

Old stone arch bridges have a rustic appeal. As Elizabeth Mock writes in *The Architecture of Bridges*: "[I]t was in stone that the building of bridges first became a conscious art, and it is therefore stone that, for better or worse, has determined many of today's attitudes towards the aesthetics of bridge design." Centuries earlier, in the third of his *Four Books on Architecture*, Italian architect Andrea Palladio observed that, whereas wooden bridges were a function of necessity, "since [men] have begun to have a regard for the immortality of their name, and when riches gave them spirit, and convenience to do greater things, they began to build [bridges] with stone, which is more durable, of greater expense, and of more glory to the builders."

Whether in the simple form of a rubble single-span arch across a small creek, or a massive railroad viaduct, or a world-class steel arch, the elegance of the geometric form of the arch bridge remains an inspiring sight, as exemplified by the variations found in New Jersey.

STONY BROOK BRIDGE

The Stony Brook Bridge, on Route 206 in Princeton Township, was built in 1792 and stands on the site of a wooden bridge that was involved in the Battle of Princeton on January 3, 1777. Near this spot just outside of the town are the ruins of Worth's Mill (seen at the left in illustration 1). V. Lansing Collins, in *Princeton: Past and Present*, notes that it was built by Joseph Worth, a Quaker who settled here in 1696. The inscription on the plaque affixed to the Stony Brook Bridge states:

> Stony Brook
> 1792
> 40 Miles to Phila
> 56 Miles to N. York

STONY BROOK BRIDGE   The dark structure at the left is what remains of the old Worth Mill. Notice the bridge's higher middle span.

General George Washington wanted to destroy the wooden bridge over Stony Brook as part of his surprise attack on the British troops at Princeton. According to historian Richard M. Ketchum's account of the battle, the American general Hugh Mercer (namesake of the county) could not complete that mission because the British, marching toward Trenton along the Post Road beyond Worth's Mill, saw the American forces, turned around, and recrossed the bridge to return to Princeton. In furious fighting, the American forces defeated the British. Then Washington had to choose between pursuing them or marching north to Morristown to regroup his forces. He decided on the latter. To delay pursuit of his army by Lord Cornwallis's British forces marching from Trenton, Washington again ordered the destruction of the bridge. The task fell to Major John Kelly, who set up artillery to fire at the British while he and his men destroyed the bridge, throwing its pieces into Stony Brook. Cornwallis brought up artillery as well and began firing. Ketchum vividly relates that "one cannonball hit a plank that Kelly was standing on, catapulting him into the icy river and doing nothing for his temper." With only the stringers (beam supports) remaining to the bridge, Kelly and his men left.

The three spans of the present bridge are composed of coursed rubble fieldstone or random coursed ashlar, with stone spandrel walls and parapets, and dressed and gauged ring stones. Such features are considered typical of the 1790s and were dominant through approximately 1850. The bridge is eighty-two feet long.

In the final report of his Stone Arch Bridge Inventory, Professor Thomas Boothby of the Department of Architectural Engineering at Pennsylvania State University makes an interesting comparison regarding the relative state of the art of bridge building in England and America at the end of the eighteenth century. In contrast to the Westminster Bridge in London, he notes, the Stony Brook Bridge, although "gracious and well-proportioned . . . reflects none of the engineering or architectural advances evident" in the Westminster Bridge, such as a lack of "low span-rise ratios and longer spans." Its "timidly proportioned" arches are evidence of what he calls "unsophisticated" construction compared with the "high state of sophistication" reflected in English and European bridge construction by around 1800. Although the sizes of these bridges are not comparable, the comparison points to the lack of real bridge-building expertise in America at the time.

The Stony Brook Bridge and the Kingston Bridge (described below) are tangible links to the Revolutionary War. Although they are not the original bridges on their sites, they replaced predecessor bridges that had the questionable distinction of having been destroyed at the personal order of General George Washington.

KINGSTON BRIDGE

Kingston is unique among New Jersey's towns in that it is philosophically, if not politically, part of three counties—Mercer, Middlesex, and Somerset—with Route 27 separating the Middlesex and Somerset sides north of the Millstone River. Originally known as King's Town, this area is in the immediate vicinity of a Lenni Lenape trail known as the Assunpink Trail, which accommodated travel between the Delaware and Raritan rivers. Kingston is identified as an established community in travelers' reports from 1675, although 1683 is considered by some to be its official settlement date. Dr. Henry Greenland opened a tavern in that year along the Millstone River. His grandson Barefoot Brunson, also a Kingston resident, was appointed the first Somerset County sheriff in 1709. In 1723 a Presbyterian church was built on the location of the present cemetery in town. By the mid-eighteenth century the town boasted a sawmill, blacksmith shop, and inns, and it served as a stagecoach stop. In colonial New Jersey, Kingston was a significant community on the King's Highway linking New York and Philadelphia.

KINGSTON BRIDGE   This winter scene conveys a sense of the landscape in the winter of 1777, when Washington and his troops passed this way and destroyed the wooden bridge here.

From about the end of the seventeenth century, the roads known as King's Highways were generally constructed by order of the colonial legislature to connect major towns. One ran from New Brunswick to Perth Amboy, another from Trenton to Elizabeth, and so on. When the Lincoln Highway was promoted by some business and civic interests early in the twentieth century to link various roads into a continuous route from New York to San Francisco, the portion of the passage through New Jersey consisted almost exclusively of the original King's Highways. From the ferry terminal in Weehawken, through Jersey City and Newark, the 3,389-mile-long Lincoln Highway carried early automobile travelers south and west across New Jersey to the Calhoun Street Bridge in Trenton and beyond. Drake Hokanson describes the Lincoln Highway in the Kingston area:

> The King's Highway had grown from an ancient Indian path, which was widened sometime after 1665 to allow passage of wagons. In places the Lincoln Highway veered from the old trail, but between New Brunswick and Trenton, the Indian trail, the King's Highway, and the original Lincoln Highway are thought to occupy very nearly the same path. Much later this route became part of U.S. 1, the major north-south road along the eastern seaboard, and when a multi-lane version of U.S. 1 was constructed to the east, the older road became a secondary route and today is New Jersey 27 and U.S. 206.

The four-span, rubble-coursed Kingston Bridge, with its barrel-shaped stone arches, is at one with the history of this place. Located just off present-day Route 27, the 110-foot-long bridge crosses the Millstone River at the dammed end of Lake Carnegie, near a historic mill building originally constructed in the late 1880s. The bridge itself was built in 1798 and is the oldest bridge in Somerset County. A more modern highway bridge now carries the Route 27 traffic, but the Kingston Bridge remains a popular fishing and photographic site adjacent to the Delaware and Raritan Canal.

A nearby plaque records that the original bridge on this site, a wooden one dating to 1705, was destroyed by Washington's troops on January 3, 1777, to delay pursuit by Lord Cornwallis following the Battle of Princeton. Nearby, at the site of the Kingston Cemetery, Washington conducted his "conference on horseback" and decided to march his men to Morristown rather than head toward New Brunswick to try to seize British supplies.

Before we leave this bridge, it is worth noting a remarkable geological association with this place. The Millstone River originally flowed south from the Sourland Mountains, but reversed direction during the Ice Age.

PRINCETON PIKE BRIDGE (MERCER STREET BRIDGE)

The Princeton Pike dates from around 1807 and carried traffic between Trenton and Kingston. The portion in Princeton is known as Mercer Street; as it travels southwest out of town, it intersects the Princeton Battlefield State Park and is considered part of the Princeton Battlefield/Stony Brook Village Historic District (although this segment did not exist at the time of the battle on January 3, 1777). From the road, travelers could see the huge tree under which the mortally wounded American general Hugh Mercer lay as the battle raged. That tree—the Mercer Oak, long the symbol of Mercer County—survived until the end of the twentieth century.

The 111-foot-long stone arch bridge that carries Princeton Pike across Stony Brook just south of the battlefield was built in 1809, more than thirty years after the Battle of Princeton. Known on the Princeton Township Master Plan as the Mercer Street Bridge, it has three rubble-coursed, barrel-shaped arches. The features that make the bridge look as if it has "socks" are icebreakers. The New Jersey

PRINCETON PIKE BRIDGE   Also known as the Mercer Street Bridge, this beautiful structure features voussoirs and icebreakers.

Historic Bridge Survey notes that the bridge is important for its role in facilitating transportation along one of the King's Highways. A narrow pedestrian bridge nearby affords an excellent opportunity to view this historic structure, which still carries traffic.

To help put the age of this bridge in perspective, we can recall that in 1809 James Madison was inaugurated as president, Robert Fulton received a patent for his steamboat, Edgar Allan Poe was born, and Thomas Paine died.

OPOSSUM ROAD BRIDGE

The Opossum Road Bridge across Beden's Brook in Montgomery Township is representative of small stone arch bridges in Somerset County and elsewhere in the central and northern parts of New Jersey. Described by the New Jersey Historic

OPOSSUM ROAD BRIDGE   Typical of rural construction, this early-nineteenth-century bridge highlights the aesthetic appeal of the stone arch and clearly shows the random rubble construction.

Bridge Survey as "a double-arched, camel-backed, random rubble bridge," it was built in 1822 by John Rowland. According to its listing on the National Register of Historic Places for engineering significance, it is the second-oldest bridge in Somerset County. The majority of such bridges in the area were constructed between 1875 and 1900.

Compare the uneven nature of the stones (the random rubble) in this bridge with the more evenly placed stones (coursed rubble) in the third of the Branch Brook bridges in Newark, discussed later in this section. Although we might think that a relatively small bridge like this would be easy to measure, different sources put it in a range from forty-seven feet (the New Jersey Historic Bridge Survey) to fifty-four feet (the Somerset County Public Information Office).

"With over 100 surviving stone bridges," nearby Hunterdon County possesses "the largest concentration of stone arch bridges in North America," according to Professor Thomas Boothby of Pennsylvania State University. The county itself claims on its Web site to have identified even more of these bridges than the New Jersey Historic Bridge Survey. These are generally short in length, and many are on private roads. Some were built in the 1930s as projects undertaken by the Depression-era Works Progress Administration (WPA). Hunterdon County maintains its own stone arch bridge inventory on its Web site and recognizes six different types, reflecting distinct styles of construction: the northern (rough stones, uncoursed spandrels, large humpbacks), the southern (dressed and shaped stones, smaller humpbacks, coursed spandrels), inset arches (with the arch within a square), skewed bridges, WPA bridges, and WPA-widened bridges.

Stone arch bridges like the Opossum Road Bridge are especially interesting because they were apparently designed and constructed by amateurs, as opposed to professional bridge builders. Perhaps because they were built by amateurs, these bridges encourage us to feel a connection to the men and women who linked their farms and communities to others in the early years of the new Republic.

NORTH BRANCH VIADUCT

Throughout the nineteenth century, competing railroads built new lines across New Jersey in hopes of capturing agricultural, industrial, and passenger business. One of the most successful lines was the Central Railroad of New Jersey (CNJ),

NORTH BRANCH VIADUCT   Note the even lines of this coursed rubble bridge.

also known as the Central New Jersey Railroad or New Jersey Central Railroad. Chartered in the mid-nineteenth century, it lasted until the Depression and ultimately became part of Conrail. CNJ was known for its famous "Blue Comet," which in its heyday in 1929 carried more than 62,000 passengers from New York to Atlantic City.

The New Jersey Transit Historic Bridge Survey describes the North Branch Viaduct as a "stunning example of stone bridges." According to that survey, this five-arch, 228-foot stone bridge was built in 1852 across the North Branch of the Raritan River, a few miles west of Raritan Borough and Somerville, to extend CNJ's lines to Phillipsburg. It carries two tracks at a width of 27 feet, and each span is 40 feet in length. The Transit Historic Bridge Survey further notes the viaduct's significance as a representative of mid-nineteenth-century railroad bridges. Interestingly, the river itself was realigned during the construction of the bridge.

One can view the bridge from River Road in North Branch and see what someone—perhaps the child or grandchild of a veteran of the American Revolution— would have seen less than a decade before the Civil War. Such is the continuing power and allure of a structure like this: it represents a kind of time machine that provides a link between generations and centuries.

ALBANY STREET BRIDGE

Originally built in 1892, the Albany Street Bridge in New Brunswick was altered in 1924, widened in 1929 and 1954, and fitted with a new deck and railings in 1985. Nonetheless, it is a good example of a large, multi-spanned, elliptical arch bridge. Structurally, the New Jersey Historic Bridge Survey describes it as having "well detailed coursed ashlar spandrel walls and gauged ring stones." The seven spans of this 595-foot-long bridge carry Albany Street, with its portion of Route 27 (also known as the Lincoln Highway), through New Brunswick and across the Raritan River to Highland Park. Nearby, another arch bridge handles Amtrak and New Jersey Transit trains along the Northeast Corridor, and still farther to the west, the John Lynch Memorial Bridge takes Route 18 across the Raritan River.

Lida Newberry notes that bridges replaced ferries at the site. The first ferry service across the Raritan River at this location was begun in 1686 by Englishman John Inian, who received exclusive rights to operate the ferry here in 1697. Newberry also indicates that Inian built a road to Trenton, known at that time as

ALBANY STREET BRIDGE   In this view looking west from Boyd Park in New Brunswick, the bridge's flattened arches seem to flow in rhythmic symmetry; the towers mark the railroad bridge just to the west.

Delaware Falls. By 1713, the community that would eventually become New Brunswick in 1730 was called Inian's Ferry, having originally been known as Prigmore's Swamp.

The ferry was replaced by a wooden bridge across the Raritan in 1776, but, like so many other bridges in this area, it was a casualty of war. On November 30, 1776, as George Washington retreated from New York toward Trenton, he ordered the bridge destroyed. After the war, notes Wheaton J. Lane, the state legislature appointed commissioners for a new bridge in 1790 and mandated that no other bridge be built nearer what was then known as Raritan Landing. This bridge was washed away by floods. The new, long (990 feet, according to John Cunningham), low-level wooden bridge that opened on November 2, 1795, ended up costing $86,695 more than originally budgeted. According to Lane, the *New Jersey Chronicle* claimed that this bridge—a "lofty structure"—"far exceeds anything of its kind in America." Perhaps the boast was not unjustified. The bridge served until it was replaced by the present bridge about a hundred years later.

GEORGIAN COURT BRIDGE

Built of brick in 1899, this fifty-foot masonry arch bridge is found on the campus of Georgian Court College, which occupies the former estate of railroad tycoon George Jay Gould (1864–1923) in Lakewood. Son of the notorious Gilded Age railroad tycoon Jay Gould, George built the estate in 1896 as his summer home.

Architect Bruce Price (1845–1903) designed the estate and the bridge. Among Price's other commissions were the famous Chateau Frontenac in Quebec City, Quebec, the American Surety Building in New York City, and the planned community of Tuxedo Park, New York. At least one source has noted that, although Price was the architect of the Georgian Court Bridge, it is likely that Gould's railroad engineers were involved in the structural design.

Price adopted the architectural style of the Georgian period in England for the structures on the Gould estate, giving rise to its name. Prominent in the latter half of the eighteenth century, Georgian architecture was a reaction to the baroque and rococo styles. Influenced by the design philosophy of Andrea Palladio, it is marked by an effort to return to classical, or Greek, aesthetic influences. The emphasis is

GEORGIAN COURT BRIDGE   The beauty of this bridge is enhanced
by its symbiosis with the courtyard and pond.

on purpose rather than decoration; columns carry the weight of buildings, rooflines are flat and horizontal, façades are long and flat, and exterior decoration is minimal. In a number of English cities, terraces of Georgian townhouses are distinguished by their similar and continuous construction. Brick was a commonly used material.

The Georgian Court Bridge was intended to carry traffic over North Lake Drive. It uses an elliptical shape, with spandrel walls, and is made of brick on timber foundations. It has terra-cotta piers, granite and marble ornaments, glazed brick detailing, and wrought-iron railings. Among its claims to fame is an appearance in the 1978 film *The Amityville Horror*. The bridge's restoration in 1999 received several awards, including the Golden Trowel Award from the International Masonry Institute as Best Restoration, 1999.

Georgian Court College was originally established as the Mount Saint Mary College and Academy in North Plainfield around 1906 by the Sisters of Mercy of New Jersey. When the college outgrew its original location, the order purchased the 155-acre Gould estate in 1924 on the condition that the institution change its name to Georgian Court. Today, this coeducational Catholic college is open to students of all faiths and describes itself as a "comprehensive college with a strong liberal arts foundation and a special concern for women."

PENNSYLVANIA RAILROAD BRIDGE

In discussing stone bridge construction by American railroad companies, photographer and author David Plowden notes that "prior to 1850 only four significant stone bridges materialized" because of their expense. However, he adds that by the mid-1850s the Reading Railroad was replacing wood with stone in its bridge construction and used masonry construction "extensively." A hiatus in stone bridge construction, caused by the advent of cheaper iron, ended in the 1880s, partly because railroad engineers were less than satisfied with the performance of the iron railroad bridges, and partly because some railroads were in better economic shape. Among the stone arch bridges constructed across the Delaware River during this revival was the eighteen-span, 1,080-foot-long Pennsylvania Railroad Bridge at Trenton, built of Clearfield sandstone between 1901 and 1903.

PENNSYLVANIA RAILROAD BRIDGE   Bridges like this give the impression that they will last forever.

William H. Brown, the chief engineer of the Pennsylvania Railroad, designed it, with W. A. Pratt and James F. Cullen, assistant engineers. (A plaque on the bridge indicates an apparent completion date of 1902 and lists Brown, Pratt, and Cullen, as well as Chas. A. Sims & Co., contractors.)

According to the application for its listing in the inventory of the National Register of Historic Places, this bridge was among those built by the Pennsylvania Railroad as part of "the most ambitious stone masonry bridge building program in the United States." Quoting a 1903 *New York Times* article, the application also notes the structure's cost—$3.5 million, including the bridge and approaches—and its reputation as "the only one in the world, with the exception of the one at New Brunswick, where four tracks run parallel." The Historic American Engineering Record (HAER) considers the crossings at Trenton important because they provided a link between New York and Philadelphia. Tracks across the Delaware were first laid in 1842 on a wooden bridge built in 1806, which was ultimately replaced by the Lower Trenton ("Trenton Makes") Bridge discussed later.

In the latter half of the nineteenth century, railroads in New Jersey competed with canals, as well as with each other, for freight. Ultimately, the canals could not survive the economic contest. Railroads then began to consolidate. At the same time, strong arch bridges were necessary to carry increasingly heavy trains from the Pennsylvania coalfields across the Delaware River and into New Jersey. As trains grew in length, power, and weight, the older wooden bridges simply could not handle them.

Three of the magnificent stone arch bridges built across the Delaware remain today and reflect the mergers and consolidations of railroads well into the twentieth century. First, the Reading Railroad (originally the Philadelphia and Reading Railroad) acquired the Central Railroad of New Jersey and built the Reading Railroad Bridge in 1875 (see color plate 6). Today this bridge, near Lower Ferry Road, is part of the Conrail line running from the Reading Terminal in Philadelphia to West Trenton. (Artist Valeri Larko created a mural of this bridge, which she calls *West Trenton Bridge*, for the Secaucus Transfer Station.) Second, the Lackawanna Railroad acquired the Morris and Essex Railroad in 1868 and constructed the Delaware River Viaduct in 1909 (described below).

The Pennsylvania Railroad acquired the Camden and Amboy Railroad (by lease) in 1871. According to Eleanore Nolan Shuman's history of Trenton, the Pennsylvania Railroad had ignored the city for some time. However, to compete with the Reading's bridge, the Pennsylvania bought land in south Trenton for the purpose of constructing its own bridge across the river. As the description in HAER explains, "when pressed by the city of Trenton to eliminate grade crossings, the PRR chose to build a new structure on a different alignment about hundred feet to the south, straightening a sharp S-curve while raising tracks above city streets." The new bridge reduced travel time to Philadelphia by twenty minutes. The first train crossed the bridge on August 23, 1903.

The Pennsylvania Railroad Bridge is now part of the Amtrak Northeast Corridor system. It was one of the last stone arch railroad bridges built in New Jersey, and it is listed in HAER as well as in Pennsylvania's Historic Architecture and Archaeology database. HAER notes that, although "the bridge's even number of spans violates classical rules of symmetry, the wide piers create three visual groupings to restore the balance." Bridges like this strong, impressive stone arch bridge hearken back to Roman construction. They give a sense of permanency to the environment and seem to conjure the ghosts of massive freight trains whistling through the night.

BRANCH BROOK PARK BRIDGES

Branch Brook Park was created in 1895 when the city of Newark transferred about sixty acres to the Essex County Park Commission to form Reservoir Park. Part of the park is on the site of Camp Frelinghuysen, where New Jersey volunteers for the Civil War assembled in 1862 to form the Thirteenth Regiment. Prominent Newark families donated additional land, and these acquisitions and other purchases doubled the park's size by 1929. Originally designed in the Romantic style, with formal gardens and arbors, the park was given a more naturalistic treatment in 1900 by landscape architect Frederick Law Olmsted (1822–1903), known nationally for his work on Central Park in New York City and the National Zoo in Washington, D.C. The Branch Brook Park Alliance claims that this was the first county park opened to the public in the United States, and it is listed on both the New Jersey and the National Registers of Historic Places.

Branch Brook Park's distinguishing features include the bridges pictured here: the Park Avenue and Bloomfield Avenue bridges, which are the largest of the park's arch spans, and the notable stone arch bridge that carries Branch Brook Park Road over a small footpath. (The park has several other small stone arch spans.)

PARK AVENUE BRIDGE   Visible are the octagonal corner piers and the concrete lampposts that enhance the distinctive appearance of this bridge in Newark's Branch Brook Park.

BLOOMFIELD AVENUE BRIDGE   The raised seals bearing the construction date add elegance to an otherwise drab-looking bridge.

The 132-foot-long Park Avenue Bridge, technically a steel arch bridge, looks more like a reinforced concrete bridge because the steel is encased in concrete. This particular style is known as the Melan-type steel arch bridge, named for Austrian engineer Joseph Melan. Melan received a patent in the United States in 1894 for a system of reinforcement using parallel iron or steel I-beams. In essence, the bridge melds an iron arch rib with the masonry arch.

The second arch bridge shown here, carrying Bloomfield Avenue over the park's main road, was built in 1904 from reinforced concrete. It is seventy feet long. The New Jersey Historic Bridge Survey comments on the simple aesthetics of this bridge; it represents a compromise between the more "ornate" section of the park to the south and the "natural rustic" portion to the north. The survey also notes the decorative raised circular concrete seals. Because such elements can have no engineering significance, they obviously reflect someone's aesthetic philosophy.

The New Jersey Historic Bridge Survey refers to the third bridge featured here as "one of the most architectonic bridges in the region," calling it "an uncommon

BRANCH BROOK
ROAD BRIDGE   This bridge reflects the style of Frederick Law Olmsted, whether or not it was designed by his firm or by the park's first landscape designers, John Bogart and N. F. Barrett.

type." It is a single-span, twenty-eight-foot-long brick arch bridge. The interior is made of brick and is now, unfortunately, covered with graffiti. Externally, the voussoirs are large and obvious, made of stone masonry that contrasts with the buff brick of the spandrel walls.

Every year in April, Branch Brook Park attracts thousands of visitors to its Cherry Blossom Festival. Like Cadwalader Park in Trenton and the better-known parks in New York and Philadelphia, Branch Brook Park offers relaxation and natural beauty to urban dwellers. The charm and aesthetic appeal of the park are enhanced by the masonry arch bridges integrated into the natural surroundings.

WASHINGTON ROAD BRIDGE

The four-span, 454-foot-long, stone-faced, reinforced concrete Washington Road Bridge is one of four arch bridges built in 1905 when the Millstone River was dammed to create an artificial lake for the Princeton crew team. According to the

WASHINGTON ROAD BRIDGE   In season, spectators can watch the Princeton crew teams from this bridge.

reminiscences of Howard Russell Butler, a Princeton University graduate (Class of 1876), the project was inspired by a conversation he had with Andrew Carnegie, the steel magnate. While painting Carnegie's portrait, Butler, former coxswain of a six-oar college barge, complained about the congestion on the Delaware and Raritan Canal, the only nearby body of water available for the Princeton team's practice. Carnegie, who had created lochs on his properties in Scotland, agreed to fund the construction of a lake, although a dispute later arose over whether he had actually promised to fund the entire cost, or simply the estimate that Butler presented to him. More embarrassing for Butler, the gift thwarted the efforts of Princeton's then president (and future New Jersey governor and U.S. president), Woodrow Wilson, to approach Carnegie for a contribution toward the new preceptorial system he was developing.

As the costs of land acquisition and construction increased, Carnegie became irritated, though he continued to fund the project. Among the design changes required to keep down costs was the substitution of stone-faced arch bridges at Washington Road and Harrison Street for the cantilever bridges originally favored by the engineers. The change of design also satisfied local government officials, who were concerned about the cost of maintaining two four-hundred-foot bridges.

According to Butler's recollections of his conversations with Carnegie, the industrialist bitterly regretted his involvement with the project:

> It was the worst thing I ever got into. It cost me $440,000. When you said $134,000, I always thought I was giving it to the college. Woodrow Wilson didn't want it and tried to get something else instead. I supposed I was to give the money first asked for, and the college would do the rest.

The bridges at Washington Road and current, replacement Harrison Street are the only two crossings over the artificial lake between the Alexander Road Bridge over Stony Brook in Princeton and the dam at the upper end of the lake in Kingston. Two other bridges, one about 140 feet in length and the other about 50 feet, were constructed at the same time in "Aqueduct Village," crossing the Millstone at Route 1 in Plainsboro. The Washington Road Bridge was built by the Hudson Engineering and Contracting Company of New York; the original Harrison Street and Route 1 bridges were built by the American Bridge Company, then part of the U.S. Steel network of companies.

Among the holdings in the archives at Princeton University are hundreds of glass plate negatives and other contemporary photographs that document the construction of Lake Carnegie and its bridges between 1905 and 1907.

DELAWARE RIVER VIADUCT

The Delaware, Lackawanna and Western Railroad (DL&W), chartered in 1851 in northeastern Pennsylvania, was best known for carrying anthracite from the Pennsylvania mines, Mike Del Vecchio writes in his *Pictorial History of American Railroads*. It was also known nationally for its advertising campaign early in the twentieth century, which featured "Phoebe Snow." This proper young lady could ride the DL&W's trains without fear for her white dress because the company's engines used clean-burning coal. With regard to its more lasting achievements, William Middleton notes that the DL&W "was the leading practitioner of reinforced concrete arch construction, with a number of major structures built between 1908 and 1915 for extensive line relocations in New Jersey and Pennsylvania."

DELAWARE RIVER VIADUCT   This image captures the sense of power and massive strength that such railroad crossings were meant to convey. Like surviving Roman viaducts, these bridges project a sense of permanence.

Among the feats accomplished by the railroad's engineers as the company expanded into northern New Jersey was the Lackawanna Cutoff, a twenty-eight-mile line built at a cost of $11 million between 1908 and 1911. William Haynes Truesdale, president of the DL&W, is said to have stood at the highest point on the existing railroad line and instructed his engineering team to build the straightest possible route through Morris, Sussex, and Warren counties. The original design of the cutoff called for two viaducts and seventy-three bridges and concrete culverts. Some 14 million cubic yards of cuts and 15 million cubic yards of fills were used to replace the more tortured route, which included the frequently flooded Manunka Chunk Tunnel. Without tight curves and steep grades, the streamlined route enabled freight trains to reach speeds up to seventy miles per hour. At its western end near Columbia, New Jersey, the cutoff approaches the nine-span, 1,450-foot-long Delaware River Viaduct, completed in 1909.

The Lackawanna Cutoff was just one part of the DL&W's overall program of expansion. David Plowden credits Lincoln Bush as the originator, in 1905, of the railroad's plan for improving its lines. Taking over from him as the railroad's chief engineer was George Ray, a leader in the use of open spandrel structures for long-span bridges. Ray influenced Abraham Burton Cohen (1882–1956), who designed the 1926 JFK Boulevard Bridge in Jersey City and who, in turn, influenced Morris Goodkind, designer of the open spandrel bridge over the Raritan River near New Brunswick that bears his name (see below). A graduate in civil engineering from Purdue University, Cohen was engineer of concrete design for the DL&W, and was also responsible for the Tunkhannock Creek Viaduct in Nicholson, Pennsylvania, an even larger railroad viaduct, built between 1912 and 1915. Plowden further notes that plans for the viaducts were supposedly drawn up by B.H. Davis, the assistant engineer for masonry design, but Cohen is acknowledged as actually having drawn the plans. William Middleton also records that Ray received the credit for designing the overall plan, but that Cohen, the specialist in concrete bridges, actually designed the bridges. Like most other endeavors, it seems, engineering is not spared its share of politics.

In the early years of the twentieth century, about ten railroad bridges crossed the Delaware between Phillipsburg and the Delaware Water Gap, primarily to facilitate the transportation of anthracite mined in Pennsylvania. Conrail abandoned the Delaware River Viaduct around 1979, and the structure is currently owned by New Jersey Transit. This bridge is important for the attention its designers paid to aesthetics as well as to engineering principles. At the end of the day, it is as close as such structures come in America to the glorious Roman viaducts of old. A view of this bridge set against the Delaware Water Gap is featured as color plate 1.

The Gap itself is perhaps one of the most extraordinary natural features in the country. Millions of years ago, as the Kittatinny Ridge was pushed upward, the Delaware River held its course in a tight S through the ridge. Geographer Charles A. Stansfield Jr. calls the Gap "one of the nation's earliest scenic attractions." Because there were few such breaks in the Appalachians, he notes, the "Delaware Water Gap was of considerable regional importance to transportation routes."

PAULINSKILL VIADUCT

The seven-span Paulinskill Viaduct at Hainesburg, New Jersey, was the second of the great bridges constructed as part of the Lackawanna Cutoff. Since Conrail abandoned the line and tore out its track in the 1970s, the Paulinskill Viaduct has taken on a bizarre and macabre life of its own. Featured in *Weird New Jersey* maga-

PAULINSKILL VIADUCT Shown here is but a small section of this massive railroad bridge along the Lackawanna Cutoff.

zine and other places, it has acquired a reputation as the "Satanic Bridge," where devil worshipers perform ceremonies in tunnels and rooms within the bridge. Legend has it that one of the workers who died while the bridge was under construction became encased in the concrete.

When it opened in 1911 (a concrete plaque gives the construction dates as 1908–1910), the Paulinskill Viaduct was the largest reinforced concrete railroad viaduct in the world, more than 1,100 feet long and 115 feet above the valley floor. Today it is possible to clamber to the top of the bridge and take in the vast panorama of northern New Jersey. On a clear day the Delaware Water Gap is visible from atop the bridge, and one can imagine the great trains roaring past.

MORRIS GOODKIND BRIDGE

At first glance, the Morris Goodkind Bridge appears to be a five-lane bridge, but it is actually two bridges side by side, spanning the Raritan River near New Brunswick. The original 1,902-foot-long, fifteen-span arch bridge was built in 1929 and named College Bridge. Designed by Morris Goodkind (1869–1968), then chief engineer of the bridge division of the New Jersey State Highway Department, it was renamed in his honor in 1969. The New Jersey Historic Bridge Survey notes that Goodkind was said to have placed particular emphasis on aesthetics in his bridge construction and considered that factor as important as the structural and engineering issues. For this design, Goodkind received the Phoebe Hobson Fowler Architectural Award from the American Society of Civil Engineers in 1930.

Like the Delaware River Viaduct and the Paulinskill Viaduct described above, the Goodkind Bridge reminds us of Roman aqueducts and viaducts. Made of reinforced concrete, the northbound bridge is striking for its six arches with open spandrels. The nine approach spans have closed spandrels. From an engineering perspective, open spandrels reduce the dead load, that is, the weight of the bridge itself. According to the New Jersey Historic Bridge Survey, this type of bridge was popular early in the twentieth century for its ability to span longer distances than could be accommodated by single-span reinforced concrete bridges, and was often used by railroads. The survey identifies the Goodkind Bridge as one of about ten open-spandrel arch bridges in the state, calling it "a bridge type that defines the

MORRIS GOODKIND BRIDGE   This view, looking west toward New Brunswick, shows the closed spandrels of the approach and the open spandrels of the arches that traverse the Raritan River.

highest level of refinement in reinforced concrete arch technology." In its impressive length and use of spandrel arches, the Morris Goodkind Bridge can be compared with the ten-span, open-spandrel, reinforced-concrete Tunkhannock Viaduct (1915) in Nicholson, Pennsylvania (mentioned above in the discussion of the Delaware River Viaduct).

The Raritan River is one of New Jersey's significant waterways. Together with its branches and tributaries, it drains an area of more than 1,100 square miles, which represents the largest river basin contained completely within the state's borders. Beginning at Budd Lake in north central New Jersey, the river travels approximately 85 miles before emptying into Raritan Bay, part of lower New York Bay.

TACONY-PALMYRA BRIDGE

A ferry service operated on the Delaware River between Tacony, Pennsylvania, and Palmyra, New Jersey, prior to the construction of a bridge. Steve Anderson's phillyroads.com Web site notes that the Tacony community was located midway between the two busy ferries that were on or near the locations of the present Benjamin Franklin and Burlington-Bristol bridges. In 1922, after nearly $200,000 was spent to construct docks and buy two ferries, the new Tacony-Palmyra service achieved great success. Apparently, however, the opening of the Benjamin Franklin Bridge in 1926 was an impetus for more bridges, despite the establishment of the Tacony ferry. Among the civic leaders who took up the idea was the founder of the Tacony-Palmyra Ferry Company, Charles A. Wright of Riverton, New Jersey. As noted by Dan Behl and other authors, Wright considered a bridge essential to the economic development of the region and later became president of the Tacony-Palmyra Bridge Company.

Ralph Modjeski designed the Tacony-Palmyra Bridge. His other notable New Jersey bridge is the Benjamin Franklin Bridge, to the south (discussed later with the suspension bridges). The Tacony-Palmyra is primarily a steel arch bridge with a through deck, but it also incorporates three-span continuous half-through tied truss spans and deck girder approach viaduct spans. (Author and engineer William Shank explains that "the tied-arch includes a tension member, or 'tie,' connecting the ends of the arch—where effective arch abutments are not available to take up the thrust.") A double-leaf bascule span rises to allow river traffic to pass. The main parabolic arch consists of top and bottom lateral truss systems; braced transverse frames hold the bottom chord points.

TACONY-PALMYRA BRIDGE   This view, looking south, captures the trussed through arch as well as the approaches and movable portion of the bridge. The double-leaf bascule is the span just to the left of the arch.

The seemingly omnipresent American Bridge Company, Steve Anderson notes, fabricated parts of the arch, bascule, and continuous truss spans at its Trenton facility. The bridge cost $4,126,000 to build. It has a total length of 3,659 feet, abutment to abutment, with the main arch span running 523 feet and the main bascule span, 247.5 feet. The arch span is 64 feet above the river. At high tide, the vertical clearance of the bascule span is 54 feet in its lowered position; the bridge must be raised for vessels requiring higher clearance.

The Tacony-Palmyra Bridge was once known as the "Nickel Bridge" because of its five-cent toll. Among the human interest stories related to the bridge is one told by Dan Behl. In 1956 Mrs. Marie Cini and her two children were stranded on the rising leaf, trapped by a barrier; all were rescued, and the traumatic episode led to the institution of safety checks on the bridge. Another, sadder piece of information concerns suicide attempts on the bridge; out of some sixty reported, eleven have been successful.

The Tacony-Palmyra Bridge, together with its sibling bridge to the north, the Burlington-Bristol Bridge, helped to make law in New Jersey with regard to the fiduciary obligations of elected officials. Pursuant to federal statute, the Tacony-Palmyra Corporation and the Burlington-Bristol Bridge Corporation, New Jersey companies, were granted authority to construct the bridges, which began operation on August 15, 1929. A group of Pittsburgh-based investors owned the bridges upon completion. In 1946 several individuals led by Clifford R. Powell, a former president of the state senate and once acting governor of New Jersey, formed a syndicate to purchase the bridges and sell them to a public agency. The extensive dealings and negotiations were kept secret from public officials until 1948, when one of the syndicate members approached a county freeholder and intimated that he had "a business transaction which would be of benefit to Burlington County." The freeholder was later advised that the two bridges were to be sold—for $12 million—to a bridge commission to be created by the freeholders, and he was told to keep the details confidential, even from his fellow officeholders.

Governor Alfred Driscoll had planned to acquire the bridges and land for the state through condemnation, a process that would have cost far less than the price paid by the county authority to the syndicate. Surprised by the county commission's action, the governor brought suit against the bridge companies to rescind the sale on the grounds that the transaction contravened public policy. Extensive litigation in a variety of courts ensued.

As with many such frauds, the story, including the legal maneuverings, is long and complex, although the motivations of greed and self-dealing are simple to understand. The decision of the New Jersey Supreme Court spends some twenty-seven of its fifty-seven pages detailing the facts. The ultimate issue in the case was whether the acquisition by the bridge commission was the result of fraud and corruption in that it was intended to benefit a few rather than the public good. The state supreme court agreed with the trial court's findings of fraud and corruption, but rejected the motion to rescind the deal. The court's remedy was to leave title to the bridges with the bridge commission, subject to judicial supervision. It also ordered the $3 million in profits to be returned. The story is remarkably and sadly analogous to the tale behind the Brooklyn Bridge, admirably detailed by David McCullough in *The Great Bridge*. What is particularly disturbing is that Powell, like "Boss" Tweed in New York, was able to prevail upon so many professionals and elected officials to abandon their duty to the public.

On a more positive note, Steve Anderson, in his comprehensive Internet feature on bridges in the New York and Philadelphia areas, quotes Harry Silcox, a local historian, on the impact of this bridge:

> The significance of the Tacony-Palmyra Bridge was that it, along with the Roosevelt Boulevard and the Market Street elevated train to Frankford, opened up the Northeast [area of Philadelphia] for settlement on a large scale. The transition was final and clear; no longer would Tacony be considered a community separate from Philadelphia. It was part of the city.

This confirmation of the local importance of the Tacony-Palmyra Bridge resonates with the theme advanced throughout this book, namely, that bridges have symbolic and social consequences that often transcend their simple utilitarian purposes.

BAYONNE STEEL ARCH BRIDGE

Until the opening of the Lupu Steel Arch Bridge in Shanghai, China, in 2003, the Bayonne Bridge (1931) was the second-longest steel arch bridge in the world (1,675 feet, center span), just behind the New River Gorge Bridge in Fayetteville, West Virginia (1,700 feet, center span; 1977), and just ahead of the Sydney Harbour Bridge (1,650 feet, center span; 1932). Constructed between 1928 and 1931 at a cost of $16 million, the Bayonne Bridge was honored as the "Most Beautiful Structure

BAYONNE STEEL
ARCH BRIDGE   Here the arch is trussed, as in the Tacony-Palmyra Bridge,
but there is no movable part to this bridge. The view is
from the Bayonne side, looking toward Staten Island.

of Steel of 1931" by the American Institute of Steel Construction. Othmar
Ammann, chief engineer of the New York Port Authority, designed the bridge,
with assistance from Leon Moisseiff (who had been involved with the Benjamin
Franklin Bridge) and architect Cass Gilbert. Ammann also designed the George
Washington Bridge and worked on others in New Jersey, such as the Goethals and
Outerbridge spans, discussed elsewhere in this book.

Writing in the early 1940s, a decade after the bridge opened, engineer David
Steinman noted that the Kill van Kull waterway handled more tonnage on an
annual basis than passed through the Suez Canal. (Steinman, incidentally, was a
bitter rival of Ammann; see Henry Petroski's *Engineers of Dreams* for details.)
Ferries had served the transportation needs here since the 1820s, and the proposed
bridge was intended to span the ferry route and so connect to streets already in
place.

The new Port Authority of New York and New Jersey, legislatively charged in
1927 to study the need for a bridge at this crossing, obviously concluded in the
affirmative. The arch form was chosen over either a three-span cantilever or a suspension bridge. Cost and aesthetics militated against a cantilever bridge at this location. The basic cost of a suspension bridge about equaled that of an arch bridge,
but the modifications needed to accommodate rail traffic involved more expense.

Moreover, geology favored the arch bridge. The abutments could be anchored in solid rock on both shores, avoiding the need to construct towers offshore for a suspension bridge.

These considerations aside, Dale Rastorfer writes that "Ammann all along had considered an arch an aesthetically superior form for the low-lying industrial landscape it would visually dominate." He further notes that Ammann, who worked under Gustav Lindenthal on the Hell Gate Bridge (1916) in New York, wanted to replicate the "expression of monumentality" of that steel through-arch bridge over the East River. His architect of choice, Cass Gilbert, prepared studies showing the stonework that would encase the structure. However, as with the George Washington Bridge, the onset of the Great Depression meant that approval was never forthcoming, and the metal abutments remain exposed.

The form of the Bayonne Bridge—a spandrel-braced arch—derives from the Hell Gate Bridge. Rastorfer quotes Ammann writing about that bridge: "The general outline of the arch with height decreasing from the center towards the ends was preserved principally for its pleasing appearance." Together with the Goethals Bridge and Outerbridge Crossing, completed a few years earlier, the Bayonne Bridge formed part of the grand plan of the Port Authority to provide an integrated transportation network around Staten Island.

The Bayonne Bridge is a through arch, also called "overhead," because the deck is suspended from a trussed arch by wire rope hangers. Steel I-beam hangers had been used in one of New Jersey's other arch bridges, the Tacony-Palmyra discussed previously, and proved unsuccessful due to vibration stresses. The Bayonne Bridge is also known as a "skew" bridge: it runs at a 58 degree angle to the water, rather than 90 degrees, to match the elevation of the existing transportation facilities on each shore. Because the War Department required that the channel be navigable at all times, even during construction, the bridge was constructed from forty separate truss segments, fabricated off-site and assembled asymmetrically. Also of interest is the participation of the American Bridge Company, which supplied the rolled steel members. They were made of carbon manganese steel— the first time such material had been used in a bridge.

Sharon Reier notes that the opening ceremonies for the Bayonne Bridge were marked by a diplomatic show of international friendship. The Australian ambassador to the United States presented a rivet from the Sydney Harbour Bridge, then under construction, to Eugenius H. Outerbridge, chairman of the Port Authority. Although the Bayonne Bridge has a longer center span, the Sydney Harbour Bridge used more than twice the tonnage of steel.

NEWARK BAY BRIDGE

The steel arch Newark Bay Bridge was built between 1954 and 1955 to relieve congestion at the Holland Tunnel, which carries traffic between Jersey City, New Jersey, and Manhattan. The bridge handles traffic to Bayonne, Jersey City, and the tunnel. Its central arch span is 1,270 feet, and when the approaches are included,

NEWARK BAY BRIDGE   This view is from the Bayonne side, looking west.

the total length is 9,560 feet. In 1995 the bridge was renamed the Vincent R. Casciano Bridge, for the New Jersey assemblyman responsible for the extension of the New Jersey Turnpike over Newark Bay.

Steve Anderson reports that the New Jersey Turnpike was a priority of Governor Alfred E. Driscoll, who persuaded legislators to create the New Jersey Turnpike Authority in 1948. A high-speed, controlled-access highway was necessary to alleviate the massive congestion on U.S. Route 1, which alone served the north-south transportation needs of the state. Interestingly, the turnpike was designed to handle traffic at a speed of 75 mph south of New Brunswick and 70 mph to the north. The speed of 60 mph was established to allow for a safety margin, and today the speed on most sections is 65 mph. The turnpike was named a Historic Civil Engineering Landmark in 2002 by the American Society of Civil Engineers.

The Newark Bay Bridge is part of the 8.2-mile Newark Bay (Hudson County) Extension of the turnpike. Built in 1954, it forms part of the link from the Holland Tunnel to Pennsylvania via Interstate 78. The bridge is similar in construction to the Delaware River–Turnpike Toll Bridge, built in 1954–1956, which carries Interstate 276 across the Delaware River from Florence Township, New Jersey, to Bristol and the Pennsylvania Turnpike (see color plate 8).

Also spanning Newark Bay near the highway bridge is a railroad lift bridge over which CSX trains pass. In color plate 3, a train waits to the left as the lift span descends into position. In the distance are the cranes of Port Elizabeth. A mural of this scene, painted by New Jersey artist Valeri Larko, hangs in the Secaucus Transfer Station along the Northeast Corridor line of the New Jersey Transit railway system.

TRUSS BRIDGES

Trusses are used to stiffen and support a bridge, and do so by distributing the loads and forces that act upon the bridge in accordance with the positioning of the members. In other words, vertical, horizontal, and diagonal "members" absorb the tensile and compressive forces. When a truss component is placed in "tension," that means that forces are trying to pull it apart; in "compression," forces are pushing it together. The members can be stiff or flexible, but the thinner they are, the less able they are to withstand compression. Members have "joints" at their ends that join them to other members to create triangular configurations, because that is the sturdiest geometric shape. Henry Petroski, in his *Engineers of Dreams*, notes that, in its simplest form, a triangular roof truss is a bridge between the walls. Horizontal "chords" are joined members, so that truss bridges generally have "upper" and "lower" chords. If there is no upper chord, we have a "pony" truss.

How the members are arranged identifies the type of truss. The king-post truss is the oldest and most basic: a single vertical member is shared by each of the triangles on either side of it. A queen-post truss has two triangles on either side of a rectangle. It allows for greater length and, in outline, is in essence a "topless" triangle. The bridges described below feature many variations on these basic types of trusses to solve specific problems of site and distance.

Truss bridges were described in the sixteenth century by Andrea Palladio in the third of his *Four Books on Architecture*. In particular, he elaborates on the construction of wooden bridges without fixing posts in the water as consisting "of beams placed cross ways, of colonelli, of cramps, and of beams placed long ways, that form the sides." In other words, he is describing a system beyond the simple plank supported by piers; instead it is a system of cross-bracing that provides the basis for truss construction.

The Swiss bridge-building brothers Johannes and Hans Ulrich Grubenmann built hybrid arch-truss bridges in the eighteenth century. Intriguingly, Petroski notes that one of those bridges was often sketched by the young Othmar Ammann. (Such links across time provide a theme that resonates throughout this book.) In the United States, the use of the truss in bridges, wood as well as iron, became very popular from the late eighteenth century onward. A myriad of styles proliferated, and many of these designs were patented. David Plowden notes that "between 1791 and 1860 as many as fifty-one bridge patents were granted, but only a dozen or so gained acceptance." The first American bridge built on the truss principle is identified by Plowden as the work of John Bliss, across the Shetucket River near Norwich, Connecticut, in the 1760s.

The early leaders of truss construction in America were Timothy Palmer (1751–1821), Lewis Wernwag (1770–1843), and Theodore Burr (1771–1822), often called the "Inspired Carpenters." Palmer was among the first American builders to cover the trusses, creating the "covered bridge." In 1805 he built the "Permanent" Bridge in Philadelphia, a 550-foot covered timber truss bridge across the Schuylkill River. Wernwag built his first bridge in 1810 across Neshaminy Creek, near Philadelphia. His third bridge, built in 1812, catapulted him to fame and proved the efficacy of truss bridges. That timber bridge—known variously as the "Colossus," the Upper Ferry, and the Fairmount Bridge—crossed the Schuylkill River at Upper Ferry, now the Fairmount section of Philadelphia. At nearly 340 feet in length, it was then the longest timber arch bridge in America. In 1806 Burr patented a truss system that used an arch brace with a multiple king-post truss. From 1812 through 1820, he was involved in the construction of no fewer than five bridges across the Susquehanna River.

Another early American architect and bridge builder, Ithiel Town (1784–1844), patented the Town lattice truss. As its name suggests, the design incorporated numerous smaller members that looked like a web. Stephen Long (1784–1864) is typical of the many bridge builders who designed a form of truss that gained popularity in certain regions of the country. Others builders were known for their work in particular materials. William Howe (1803–1852), for example, combined wooden compression members on the diagonals with vertical iron tensile members.

Although early American bridge builders like Palmer, Burr, and Wernwag were highly successful, their bridges were based more on intuition and rule of thumb than scientific principle. Until the publication of treatises by the influential American engineer Squire Whipple (1804–1888) and the rise of engineering schools in the mid-nineteenth century, bridges were not built with mathematical precision. Hybrids were common, such as the "camelback" or "hump" bridges that combined arch and truss. Whipple sought to quantify the science of bridge construction in *A Work on Bridge Building* (1847). He held two patents, one issued in 1841 for an iron truss bridge, and the second in 1872 for an improvement in lift drawbridges. He also designed a trapezoidal form of truss. His enthusiasm for the truss is apparent in his conclusion to U.S. Patent No. 2064 (April 24, 1841): "[I]t is obvious that with arrangement, truss bridges will be more secure from the lateral deflection of their trusses and consequently may be used with safety of a greater span than when no such precaution is taken to prevent lateral flexure." Whipple's work on the first large-scale railroad iron bridge, for the Rensselaer and Saratoga Railroad, set the standard for future truss bridges with its inclined end posts (as opposed to vertical members perpendicular to the lower chord) and cylindrical pins connecting the members. Whipple is considered to be the first American engineer to analyze bridge construction systematically from a mathematical and scientific perspective in order to evaluate stress.

Some of the more prevalent types of trusses are listed below, with a few examples featured in this book:

1   The Town truss, patented by Ithiel Town in 1820. Latticework forms trusses that do not rely on an arch to sustain support.

2   The Haupt truss, patented by Herman Haupt in 1839. The end panels and the abutments absorb the compressive forces, and the cross bracings are more elongated in the panels.

3   The Howe truss, patented by William Howe in 1840 (see the Green Sergeant's Bridge). Iron, instead of wood, is used for the vertical members of the truss; wood forms the X portion of each segment or panel. Variations include (1) the Howe truss with counter braces and (2) the Howe truss with wooden bracing and iron rods.

4   The Pratt truss, invented by the architect Caleb Pratt and his son Thomas, an engineer, in 1844 (see the Calhoun Street Bridge and the New Hope–

Lambertville Bridge). It combines elements of the queen-post truss with the king-post truss and uses iron for the X portion of each panel, in contrast to the Howe truss. This design was modified by C. H. Parker to form a "camelback" configuration, where the top chord arches and is not parallel with the bottom chord. The Baltimore Pratt truss provides additional vertical bracing within the panels, and the Pennsylvania Pratt truss is an arched configuration with Baltimore-type vertical braces.

5   The Warren truss, patented in 1846 by James Warren and a partner. This design is based on the isosceles triangle (see the Uhlerstown-Frenchtown Bridge and the Upper Black Eddy–Milford Bridge). Variations include: a Burr-type arch; additional and tighter diagonal and vertical chords (the subdivided Warren truss; see the Lower Trenton Bridge); additional diagonal members (the double Warren truss; see the Washington Crossing Bridge and the Riverton-Belvidere Bridge); and even more concentrated diagonal bracing (the quadri-lateral Warren truss).

6   The Bollman truss, invented by Wendell Bollman, first built in 1850 and patented in 1852. This design uses cast and wrought iron.

7   The lenticular truss, invented in Germany by Friedrich August von Pauli (1802–1883). Otherwise known as the Pauli truss after the design was published in 1865, it became known as lenticular because of the lens shape of the truss (see the Neshanic Station Bridge). Pauli's intent was to combine the advantages of a suspension bridge in dealing with load factors, based on the opposing arches, with willow tree–like flexibility of a truss framework (as opposed to cables). Gustav Lindenthal modified the Pauli truss for his first important design, the famous Smithfield Street Bridge in Pittsburgh.

8   The Fink truss, invented by Albert Fink in the 1860s. This form was used mostly for railroad bridges.

MUSCONETCONG BRIDGE

The first known cast-iron bridge, completed in 1779 in Shropshire, England, was a one-hundred-foot arch bridge across the Severn River, built by Thomas Pritchard (the Coalbrookdale Bridge). In the United States, the first cast-iron bridge crossed Dunlap's Creek, near Pittsburgh, in 1839. Later, wrought iron became a popular

MUSCONETCONG BRIDGE   It is easy to overlook the charm of historic
bridges such as this.

material for bridge construction. New Jersey can boast of several historic cast-iron and wrought-iron bridges that are significant nationally.

The Musconetcong Bridge (also known on the National Register of Historic Places as the New Hampton Pony Pratt Truss Bridge), was built in 1868 by William and Charles Cowin. It is eighty-five feet long and carries Shoddy Mill Road over the Musconetcong River in New Hampton. The Cowin Works of Lambertville was also responsible for the West Main Street Bridge in Clinton, New Jersey, and the School Street Bridge in nearby Glen Gardner. According to the New Jersey Historic Bridge Survey, this pony Pratt truss bridge is one of the most significant in New Jersey because it demonstrates "the transition from wood to metal truss spans" and because it is the oldest of the three such spans in the area. It features wrought-iron tension members and cast-iron compression members.

The engineer was Francis Lowthrop (1810–1890; sometimes spelled Lowthorp), who also supervised the West Main Street and School Street bridges. Beyond New Jersey, he oversaw the Riverside Avenue Bridge, built in 1871, which is the only extant cast-iron truss bridge in Connecticut. As the base for that bridge, Lowthrop used the Whipple truss, with some improvements of his own. According to a survey of historic bridges by the University of Florida (credited to Perry

Green), the Riverside Avenue and School Street bridges are among seventy-four surviving bridges in the United States that have major structural members made of cast and wrought iron.

The Musconetcong River commences in Lake Musconetcong and flows approximately forty-three miles to meet the Delaware River at Riegelsville, New Jersey. In their charming book *Exploring the Little Rivers of New Jersey*, James and Margaret Cawley consider it "one of the most interesting rivers in New Jersey," not least because it served as an important feeder to the engineering miracle that was the Morris Canal.

WEST MAIN STREET BRIDGE

This 170-foot pony Pratt through-truss bridge, built in 1870 by William Cowin of Lambertville to cross the South Branch of the Raritan River, has become an integral

WEST MAIN STREET BRIDGE   This popular feature of Clinton's town center shows off the artistry and beauty of ornate wrought iron.

feature of the town of Clinton. Like the nearby Musconetcong and School Street bridges, also fabricated by Cowin, it is a significant example of cast- and wrought-iron construction. Unlike its companion one-span bridges, however, this bridge has two spans and is pin-connected.

The West Main Street Bridge was engineered by Francis C. Lowthrop, who was also known for his railroad bridges and who patented various methods of using cast iron in bridges in the mid-nineteenth century. Here the cast-iron members are for compression, and the wrought-iron ones for tension. According to the New Jersey Historic Bridge Survey, Lowthrop favored cast iron because, in his words, "there is much more to be feared from defects in wrought iron used for tensile than for cast iron used for compressive purposes." Apparently he had conducted experiments to determine the ability of wrought iron to handle these forces. This innovative bridge engineer is buried in Riverview Cemetery in Trenton.

The New Jersey Historic Bridge Survey points out an unusual feature of the West Main Street Bridge: "the patented Johnson tightener, an eccentric ratchet and pawl arrangement at the panel point for tuning the bridge," that is, to perform maintenance on the bridge by keeping the members secure. The floor beams are considered unusual "in the use of two rods in an inverted Kingpost truss arrangement which may be adjusted to increase tension." On the basis of "its age, use of materials, design, and documentation," the authors of the survey regard the West Main Street Bridge as "one of the most important bridges in the nation." Thus, more than 125 years ago, the engineering and construction team of Lowthrop and Cowin produced three bridges in central New Jersey that rank among the more historically significant in the nation.

——————— SCHOOL STREET BRIDGE

Like its companions, the Musconetcong Bridge in New Hampton and the West Main Street Bridge in Clinton, this eighty-four-foot pony Pratt truss bridge in Glen Gardner was engineered by Francis Lowthrop and built by the foundry of William and Charles Cowin of Lambertville. It, too, is constructed of wrought and cast iron, and is one of the relatively few such bridges still standing in the United States. For these reasons, it is deemed to be "of national importance" by the New Jersey Historic Bridge Survey. David Plowden notes that "the Pratt system has the further

SCHOOL STREET BRIDGE   This striking pony truss (a truss without
the top horizontal chord) is a beautiful work
of craftsmanship.

distinction of having been the only truss form to have been executed in wood, iron, and steel," and he singles out the School Street, Musconetcong, and West Main Street bridges as three examples of the now rare "early metal Pratt trusses."

This bridge was built in 1870 to carry School Street across Spruce Run River. Its surroundings include a nineteenth-century mill. The town of Glen Gardner grew up in the area of a tavern established in 1760. According to the *Encyclopedia of New Jersey*, one of the town's early names was Sodom, owing to the inhabitants' "indifference to a wandering evangelist."

ROSEMONT–RAVEN ROCK ROAD BRIDGE

Hunterdon County, which claims to have more stone arch bridges than any comparable area in the United States, is also home to this 129-foot-long, nine-panel, pin-connected Pratt through-truss bridge crossing Lockatong Creek in Delaware

Township. It was built in 1878 by the Lambertville Iron Works, a firm originally founded in 1849 as Laver and Cowin (it changed names in 1878). William Cowin, the head of the company, was also involved with the three cast- and wrought-iron bridges engineered by Francis Lowthrop for Clinton, Glen Gardner, and New Hampton, discussed earlier. (Lowthrop is not identified as having any involvement with this bridge.) Like the West Main Street Bridge in Clinton, the Rosemont–Raven Rock Road Bridge has a center ring to which the bottom lateral bracings are connected.

According to the New Jersey Historic Bridge Survey, this bridge is "one of the most important thru truss bridges in the state based on its age, nearly complete state of preservation, and use of Phoenix columns for the compression members."

ROSEMONT–RAVEN ROCK
ROAD BRIDGE

At one time, what we now consider to be back roads were significant thoroughfares that warranted the construction and expense of attractive bridges.

The Phoenix column is described by the survey as a "wrought iron segmental channel riveted together to form a tube of great compressive strength." The influential engineer J.A.L. Waddell noted that this innovation was "a great factor causing the substitution of wrought iron for cast iron in compression members of pin-connected bridges." (The Phoenix Bridge Company is discussed in more detail in connection with the Calhoun Street Bridge.)

Thirty years ago, in his book *The Passaic River*, Norman Brydon cited an iron bridge over the Passaic at New Providence as "[o]ne of the last of the fast-disappearing iron bridges." Surviving structures like the Rosemont–Raven Rock Road Bridge, once commonplace in the New Jersey landscape, have now achieved special status.

JACOBS CREEK (BEAR TAVERN ROAD) BRIDGE

Built by the King Iron Bridge and Manufacturing Company in 1882, the 75-foot-long steel Jacobs Creek Bridge on Bear Tavern Road in Hopewell Township is the oldest through-truss bridge in Mercer County, according to the New Jersey Historic Bridge Survey. Moreover, it is significant as a surviving example of a now rare bridge type. Although the pin-connected Pratt truss was very common in the late nineteenth century, this particular bridge is a Pratt half-hip. Popular from the 1890s through the early twentieth century, this variation is distinguished by inclined end posts that do not reach the length of the entire panel. Another example in New Jersey is the bridge carrying Preventorium Road over Manasquan Creek in Howell, Monmouth County; that bridge was built in 1899 by the Wrought Iron Bridge Company, which was also responsible for the Nevius Street Bridge discussed below.

The King Iron Bridge and Manufacturing Company was founded in Cleveland, Ohio, in the mid-nineteenth century by Zenas King, who patented a tubular bowstring bridge that became a national success. Despite its popularity, the design is represented by fewer than six surviving bridges in New Jersey, including one from 1885 on Mine Road in Hopewell, and a pedestrian drawbridge in River Edge, Bergen County, which is reputed to be the oldest standing King Iron bridge in the country.

JACOBS CREEK
(BEAR TAVERN ROAD) BRIDGE   According to the Historic Bridge Survey,
nineteenth-century metal bridges such as
this one are a vanishing type.

Not far from the Jacob's Creek Bridge, the Mine Road Bridge in Hopewell crosses Stony Brook. Like its neighbor, this 102-foot Pratt half-hip through-truss bridge has true floor-beam hangers, lateral bracing connections, and pronglike floor beam connectors at the verticals.

CALHOUN STREET BRIDGE

Although the Calhoun Street Bridge may be second to the "Trenton Makes" (Lower Trenton) Bridge in the hearts of Trenton bridge lovers—some of whom, however, might admit that it does surpass that bridge in their affections—it is in some ways more famous and historic. Calhoun Street was first known as Beatty's

Ferry Road, one of the settlement's original streets. As the name suggests, one of Trenton's two ferries operated here, and the original wooden bridge on this site replaced the Kirkbride-Rutherford Ferry. That bridge was completed in 1861 after almost two years of construction—and more than two decades after the state legislature authorized it. It survived until 1884, when it was destroyed by a fire believed to have been caused by a lit cigar butt.

The present bridge was built on the first bridge's piers and abutments by the Phoenix Bridge Company of Phoenixville, Pennsylvania. In contrast to its predecessor, this approximately 1,273-foot-long bridge was finished within sixty days by eighty-three workmen using 730 tons of wrought iron, and opened on October 20, 1884. A Pratt through-truss bridge, it uses seven spans (each nearly 180 feet long) to connect Trenton to Morrisville, Pennsylvania.

Once known as the Trenton City Bridge, or just City Bridge, this structure was featured in an 1885 catalog of the Phoenix Bridge Company as one of the most advanced bridges in the country. The company's emphasis on aesthetics is notable in view of our contemporary interest in the subject: "The sidewalk railing serves the double purpose of a guards and trussed stringed for a portion of the sidewalk load. With its lines plainly expressive of the purpose of its construction, it materially contributes to the light and graceful, yet most substantial, appearance of the entire structure."

CALHOUN STREET BRIDGE   A simple and elegant bridge, it conveys a sense of lightness.

The Phoenix Bridge Company was one of the preeminent bridge-building firms in the country in the nineteenth century. According to its 1885 catalog, the company began "on a small scale" in 1790 and manufactured wrought-iron field guns during the American Civil War. In 1862 it introduced its proprietary "Phoenix column," and it began manufacturing eyebars in 1866. Both the column and the eyebars were designed to resist "the strains of compression and tension." According to the company, they have "performed signal service in developing the American type of bridge, and have made practicable the rapid and economical manufacture of engineering structures adapted to a great variety of purposes." The company approved of the Pratt wood and Whipple iron trusses, and used those as the basis for its designs.

One of the more intriguing features of the Calhoun Street Bridge is a plaque that still points to San Francisco and New York, reflecting its former glory as part of the transcontinental Lincoln Highway route developed in 1912 to promote the automobile industry. By 1928, when the Calhoun Street Bridge was acquired by the Joint Commission for Eliminating Toll Bridges, it also contained trolley tracks.

Although today the comparison might raise some eyebrows, Eleanore Shuman relates that "Trenton was often compared to Venice, in a small way, because its many waterways, numerous bridges, and irregular, wandering streets gave the town an appearance of antiquity and quaintness which prompted many people to see in it a likeness to the Italian city." Despite the many changes the city has undergone over the decades, the Calhoun Street Bridge remains a unique and historic crossing.

NEVIUS STREET BRIDGE

The 150-foot wrought-iron Nevius Street Bridge, built in 1886 across the Raritan River in Raritan Borough, is representative of long-span highway and railroad bridges constructed in the latter half of the nineteenth century. Moreover, the New Jersey Historic Bridge Survey calls it a rare surviving example of the double-intersection Pratt truss, whereby additional diagonal members extend across two panels of the normal Pratt truss. The bridge is also representative of the use of wrought iron in the relatively limited period of iron bridge construction before the dominance of steel. The authors of the state bridge survey go so far as to say that "metal trusses like the Nevius Street Bridge represent a noteworthy period of economic and industrial development in the country's history, and played a prominent part in the advance of a reliable network of overland transportation."

Succeeding a wood bridge that had stood at this site since the mid-1840s, the Nevius Street Bridge was built by the Wrought Iron Bridge Company of Canton, Ohio. This company was also responsible for one portion of the Higginsville Road Bridges over the South Branch of the Raritan River in Hillsborough, discussed elsewhere.

Bridges are about connections, and this one offers a story as compelling as any in this book. A family named Nevius is known to have lived in this area as early as the mid-1700s. Research into available genealogical records indicates that Johannes Nevius was born in 1740 in Brooklyn and died in November 1788 in Whiteside,

NEVIUS STREET BRIDGE   The double-intersection Pratt truss is clearly shown, with the diagonal bracing going from the upper right to the lower left of the panel (the basic Pratt truss), and the second diagonal going from the same upper right corner across the second panel.

Somerset County, New Jersey. His father, apparently widowed, married Susanna Martense Schenck in Raritan Landing, Somerset County, in 1764. This family traces its lineage back to the Reverend Matthias Nevius, born in Holland around 1599. Another genealogy Web site refers to a Johannes Neffius, born in 1550 in Antwerp, Belgium, as possibly the first known Nevius ancestor; a second generation of that family included Johannes Nevius, born in 1594 in Zoelen, Holland. The same source follows a fifth generation, which counted David Peter Nevius, who lived in Franklin Township, Somerset County, in the eighteenth century, as well as Johannes Nevius, husband of Susanna Martense Schenck. So when crossing this bridge, a significant example of wrought-iron construction in its own right, consider the connections that reach back more than four hundred years to Holland and the age of Rembrandt.

In 2004, while this book was in production, the Nevius Street Bridge was permanently closed to traffic owing to structural weaknesses. A parallel structure at Lyman Street will eventually carry traffic over the Raritan River. The Nevius Street Bridge is slated for rehabilitation as a pedestrian-only crossing.

MAIN STREET (CALIFON) BRIDGE

The one-hundred-foot Main Street Bridge was built in 1887 by I. P. Bartley and Company across the South Branch of the Raritan River in Califon. Originally designed as a steel Pratt through-truss bridge, it was renovated and widened in 1985 with rolled I-section steel stringers added under the trusses. Therefore, technically, it is now a beam bridge and can no longer be called a true truss bridge. Nonetheless, the truss superstructure was left in place, and it contains some steel fabric with the "Carnegie" stamp on it. Because the Main Street Bridge was originally a Pratt through-truss—and still looks like one—it is included here. It is one of those bridges that truly adds to the beauty of the landscape of which it is a part.

Notwithstanding the alteration, the New Jersey Historic Bridge Survey recommended this structure for historic status. It is significant as one of the fewer than five bridges built by the prominent Mount Olive–based Bartley Company. (One is in the Great Swamp.) The area of Bartley, originally called Bartleyville, reflects the firm's importance. This attractive bridge had significant utilitarian

MAIN STREET (CALIFON) BRIDGE   One of the prettiest bridges of its kind, it stands out in this attractive river and woods setting.

functions as well, affording the surrounding farming community access to the Califon railroad station. The town itself, according to the *Encyclopedia of New Jersey*, was originally named California, in honor of a resident who returned from the California gold rush in 1850, but the townspeople could not fit all the letters on the sign for their train station.

HIGGINSVILLE ROAD BRIDGES

The structure that carries Higginsville Road across the South Branch of the Raritan River in Hillsborough looks like a single bridge, but in fact, it is considered to be two separate bridges, one following the other. They survive in excellent condition as representatives of the Pratt truss. The older one (seen in the background in the photograph), built in 1890 by Milliken Brothers of New York, is a 102-foot-long Pratt half-hip bridge. It has seven panels and is pin-connected. The New Jersey Historic Bridge Survey notes that it is not only "one of the most complete examples of the popular late-nineteenth-century bridge type in the region," but also "a rare example of the New York City fabricator Milliken Bros.," which was active from 1887 until 1907.

The Milliken firm was established by the brothers Foster (a structural engineer) and Edward. The predecessor company founded by their father, Milliken, Smith and Company, was an agent for the Phoenix Iron Works. The brothers seem to have followed the example of many nineteenth-century bridge builders, learning their trade at other companies and then setting out to establish their own design and manufacturing firm. In 1905–1906 the company was responsible for the foundations and metal construction of the Palace of Fine Arts in Mexico City.

HIGGINSVILLE ROAD BRIDGES Bridges like these seem to appear in the middle of nowhere in New Jersey, and hearken back to the great age of bridge construction.

The newer, more southerly portion of the Higginsville Road Bridges (pictured in the foreground) was designed and built in 1893 by the Wrought Iron Bridge Company of Canton, Ohio, one of the first wrought-iron truss manufacturers. (In the photograph, the name "Wrought Iron Bridge Company" is clearly visible on the bridge entrance.) Like its companion, this 103-foot-long bridge also has seven panels and is a pin-connected Pratt half-hip through-truss. The Wrought Iron Bridge Company was formed in 1864 and made different types of truss bridges, which were showcased in its catalog. Another of the company's structures featured in this book is the Nevius Street Bridge. The American Bridge Company acquired the firm in 1900.

In 2000 the Higginsville Road Bridges were added to the National Register of Historic Places.

NESHANIC STATION BRIDGE

The 285-foot, two-span Neshanic Station Bridge, built by the Berlin Bridge Company of Connecticut in 1896 across the South Branch of the Raritan River in Branchburg, is one of the most attractive bridges in the state. To this author's knowledge, it is one of only two lenticular bridges in New Jersey. Here, although the design is lenticular (lenslike), the bridge is a variation of the Pratt truss configuration. The New Jersey Historic Bridge Survey has identified a pony form of this bridge, the Bear Swamp Road Bridge (1888) over the Ramapo River in Bergen County, also built by the Berlin Bridge Company. (A pony bridge lacks horizontal bracing over the top chords and generally serves shorter spans.)

Trusses with an oval shape were a hallmark of the Berlin Bridge Company, which sold these bridges nationally. According to the Web site "Lenticular Truss Bridges," the Berlin Bridge Company built at least four hundred truss bridges, although the number of lenticular ones is not certain. This source also claims that approximately fifty lenticular truss bridges remain around the country. Alan Lutenegger and Amy Cerato of the University of Massachusetts Department of Civil and Environmental Engineering claim that almost eight hundred lenticular truss bridges were constructed in the United States by the Berlin Bridge Company. The Connecticut Historic Highway Bridges Web site contends that, in its heyday, the Berlin Bridge Company "was probably the largest structural fabricator in New

England." In 1900 the company merged with the American Bridge Company, owned by J. P. Morgan, who was seeking control over the structural fabricating industry. The American Bridge Company was one of the major suppliers to state and local bridge authorities at the beginning of the twentieth century. It was acquired by U.S. Steel in 1904.

The lenticular design was patented in the United States in 1878 by William O. Douglas of Binghamton, New York (not to be confused with the Supreme Court justice), although it was invented in Germany by Friedrich August von Pauli. Because of their shape, lenticular trusses are sometimes called "fish belly trusses" or "parabolic trusses." Douglas's patent refers to an "elliptical truss." The engineering of the bridge succeeds, according to the author of "Berlin Iron Bridges in Connecticut," because "the lenticular functions to transfer loads on the deck of the bridge out to the ends, which rest on solid abutments." The effect of the curved chords on top and bottom made the truss deepest in the center, where the greatest strength was necessary. Although this configuration required less iron, the bridge was nonetheless more costly to manufacture because of the multiple angles. These bridges were built to last, however. Until the 1890s, the material of choice, as with other truss bridges, was wrought iron. Even when steel construc-

NESHANIC STATION BRIDGE   Viewing the only full lenticular truss bridge in New Jersey is like gazing upon a mathematical equation.

tion took over, the Berlin Bridge Company continued to use wrought iron for most of its bridges. Pinned, as opposed to riveted, connections were employed to join portions of the bridge.

In his patent application, Douglas claimed to have invented new and useful improvements in truss bridges, having as his object "to improve the construction and efficiency of truss bridges by combining as far as possible the maximum strength with the minimum of cost." To this end, his design consisted, "first, in the combination of parts forming an elliptical truss; and, secondly, in the construction of bridges with such trusses." He further noted that "all the tensile members may be made of any convenient form—round, square, or flat and all compressive members must be constructed with a proper ratio of diameter to the length, in order to properly resist compressive strain. The trusses or bridge may be constructed of iron or wood, or both." Like many foreign authors and inventors in an era without solid treaty protection for intellectual property, the unfortunate Pauli could not protect his intellectual property rights in this design in the United States.

WARD STREET BRIDGE

When the Marquis de Lafayette visited Hightstown, the story goes, he misheard its name as Icetown and so referred to it that way. Founded by John and Mary Hights in the mid-eighteenth century, the town saw its prominence vanish in the second half of the twentieth century as suburban communities sprang up around it. Fortunately, Hightstown and the many New Jersey towns that suffered a similar fate are beginning to make a comeback. Main streets are improved, enlivened with local businesses, and offer a focal point for the surrounding developments. In the case of Hightstown, the 254-foot, two-span Ward Street Bridge provides a kind of rallying point in connection with Peddie Lake and the center of town. The bridge is easily visible from the dammed area of the lake, which was formed by damming Rocky Creek, a tributary of the Millstone River. It once served as John Hights's millpond. Hightstown is also home to the Peddie School, a private school founded in 1864. Among the impressive Victorian homes on Stockton Street is the Mary Norton House, where Clara Barton visited in 1862.

WARD STREET BRIDGE   This late-nineteenth-century bridge stands as an elemental component of Hightstown, known for its Victorian homes.

Built in 1896 by the New Jersey Steel and Iron Company, the Ward Street Bridge is considered a rare bridge type: a double-intersection Warren truss with hangers. Founded in 1846 as the Trenton Iron Company, the New Jersey Steel and Iron Company was acquired by the American Bridge Company in 1901.

DINGMAN'S FERRY BRIDGE

The Dingman's Ferry Bridge is said to be one of only sixteen privately owned toll bridges in the country, and the only one in New Jersey. It occupies the site of a ferry service begun in 1735 by Andrew Dingman. The Dingman family prospered here; one descendant, "Judge" Daniel W. Dingman, held court on the Pennsylvania side in what became known as Dingman's Choice. In 1836 the family (through the Dingman's Choice and Delaware Bridge Company, chartered in 1834) built the first bridge on the site, a wooden covered bridge, between Dingman's, Pennsylvania, and Sandyston Township, New Jersey. (As often happens, various chroniclers give conflicting information about the date of the bridge and the names of the people involved; see Norman Brydon and Frank Dale for different interpretations of the sources. The New Jersey Historic Bridge Survey claims to have consulted "owners' records." An "official" Web site for the bridge can be found at www.dingmansbridge.com.)

The covered bridge was destroyed in the flood of 1846 when the upriver Milford Bridge broke free, crashed into it, and carried it away. The second bridge on the site, also a covered bridge, was built in 1850 and destroyed by a tornado in 1853. The ill luck continued with the Dingmans' third bridge, which collapsed within four years of its construction in 1856. The Dingmans blamed the construction company and restored their ferry service. In 1900 the bridge franchise was sold at a tax sale to James, Will, and E. A. Perkins, who in that year opened the present wrought-iron bridge across the Delaware River from Sandyston, New Jersey, to Delaware Township, Pennsylvania. It is a pin-connected, three-span Baltimore through truss and uses Phoenix columns. Supposedly, the bridge was built around 1890 at Laceyville, Pennsylvania, and moved to the present site in 1900. The bridge has a minimum clearance over the water of approximately thirty feet.

DINGMAN'S FERRY BRIDGE   A view from the New Jersey side.

NEW HOPE–LAMBERTVILLE BRIDGE

Lambertville and New Hope, like Buda and Pest, essentially form one city with a river through the center. Like many places along the Delaware River, the two sides were originally served by a ferry—Coryell's Ferry—established in the early eighteenth century. According to Norman Brydon, Lambertville was known at one time as "Bungtown" because of its taverns and brawls. Wheaton J. Lane observes that taverns were no accident in the vicinity of ferry crossings, where travelers often faced long waits. Lambertville was a significant stagecoach stop, and the popular Lambertville House still welcomes travelers on Bridge Street. Also located on Bridge Street is the home of James Wilson Marshall, who left left Lambertville in 1834 and discovered gold at Sutter's Mill in California in 1848.

The first bridge at this site was a wooden covered bridge designed and built in 1814 by Lewis Wernwag. It was 1,051 feet long, had six arched spans, and served until 1841. A second covered bridge, built in 1842, was destroyed in the 1903 flood that damaged other Delaware River crossings. The present bridge was built in 1904 as a six-span, pin-connected Pratt through truss. It is about 1,045 feet long, with even span lengths of about 171 feet each. Astoundingly, as reported by the Dela-

NEW HOPE–LAMBERTVILLE BRIDGE   From the Lambertville side, the diagonals of the Pratt truss are seen.

ware River Joint Toll Bridge Commission, this bridge cost $63,818.81, less than the $67,936.37 needed to build the original bridge in 1814.

The demise of the ferry also brought a new name to the location, according to John Cunningham in *This Is New Jersey*. U.S. Senator John Lambert had a post office established there and had the town name changed to Lambert's Ville in 1812, triggering cries of "Lambert's villainy" from Coryell descendants.

Today, Lambertville and New Hope are known for their antique shops and art galleries. The bridge connecting them, which at one time handled wagons and trolleys, contains a pedestrian walkway, from which Bowman's Tower in Washington Crossing State Park on the Pennsylvania side can be observed. The bridge is also known for the swallows that make it their home.

WASHINGTON CROSSING BRIDGE

This is hallowed ground. Here, at McKonkey's Ferry, General George Washington crossed the Delaware River on Christmas Day 1776, marched his men south to Trenton to surprise the Hessian brigade there, and secured a military and morale turning point in the American War for Independence.

The three divisions of Washington's army were spread out along the Pennsylvania side of the Delaware, from Coryell's Ferry (Lambertville) to Trenton Ferry (in the middle) to Dunk's Ferry (toward Bordentown). The main force was camped between Coryell's Ferry and, to the south, McKonkey's Ferry. The names of the American officers, including Brigadier General James Ewing and Colonel John Cadwalader, reverberate in nearby locations today (Ewing Township and Cadwalader Park in Trenton).

Washington made the urgency of the young nation's situation clear to John Hancock on December 20: "ten days more will put an end to the existence of our army." Washington planned to cross 2,400 men at McKonkey's Ferry, march to Trenton, and then on to Princeton and New Brunswick. The crossing was made in large black Durham boats, river freight haulers forty to sixty feet in length. Under cover of darkness, Washington's army completed the crossing around four in the morning and split into two wings to march on Trenton. The two forces attacked from different sides at almost the same time, and Trenton was taken.

WASHINGTON
CROSSING BRIDGE   This rather narrow bridge, painted blue, is an
enduring and endearing feature of the historic site.
The X configuration of the double Warren truss is
clearly seen.

The ferry at this site was originally known as Johnson's Ferry. William McKonkey, son of the ferry owner in Washington's day, ran a tavern on the New Jersey side, which still stands. The first bridge here, a wooden one built in 1831–1834, was an 875-foot-long six-span covered bridge. It was destroyed by a flood in 1841. The covered bridge built to replace it was also a victim of flood in 1903. The current bridge, built in 1904, is a riveted-steel double Warren through truss. Five of its six spans are 143 feet in length, and one is 137 feet, for a total length of nearly 877 feet. The bridge was repaired following severe damage by flood in 1955, and in 1994 it was significantly rehabilitated.

Count yourself lucky if you visit the site and do not overhear yet another tourist ask why Washington did not simply take the bridge.

UHLERSTOWN-
FRENCHTOWN BRIDGE

To connect Frenchtown, New Jersey, to Uhlerstown, Pennsylvania, the Alexandria Bridge Company built the first bridge on this site between 1842 and 1843, a wooden covered bridge with Town-type latticed trusses. It stood until the great flood of 1903 carried away the two spans that were closest to New Jersey. The piers and abutments of that original bridge support the current one, built in 1905. This bridge was completely remodeled in 1931 to accommodate traffic demands. The superstructure was replaced with steel, a wood floor, and a sidewalk. In 1949 a grilled steel floor replaced the wood deck.

Uhlerstown was a significant commercial center from about 1832 to around 1932 as a result of its location on the Delaware Division of the Pennsylvania Canal. Originally called Mexico, the town was renamed in 1871 for its postmaster, Michael Uhler. President Grover Cleveland is said to have visited here once. Across the river, Frenchtown supposedly took its name after a family of refugees fleeing from the French Revolution settled there. Frenchtown was a significant railroad stop on the Belvidere Delaware Railroad, and the bridge linked Uhlerstown to that railroad. Today, like Lambertville to the south, Frenchtown is known for its antique shops and art galleries, and for the recreational activities along the Delaware and Raritan Canal Feeder towpath, which passes through the town.

UHLERSTOWN-
FRENCHTOWN BRIDGE   Notice how high above the water this bridge stands—a wise precaution, given the long history of bridges destroyed by floods on the Delaware River.

The present bridge, rebuilt in 1931 as a riveted-steel Warren through truss, is nearly 950 feet long. Five of its six spans are 156 feet in length, and one is 152 feet. It is interesting to compare this bridge with the New Hope–Lambertville Bridge (1903) to note the difference between riveted and pin-connected design. James L. Garvin explains that pin-connected joints are representative of an older design, generally used not later than 1900, which required less mathematical exactitude. The pin—a threaded bolt—connected joints and provided some flexibility. The riveted plate reflects a later, more advanced truss design and does not have the pin's flexibility.

To the north of Frenchtown is the Upper Black Eddy–Milford Bridge, built in 1933 as a three-span, riveted-steel Warren truss in a camelback configuration (see color plate 7). A guide to non-toll bridges published by the Delaware River Joint Toll Bridge Commission reports that the original ferries at this site were the Lowrytown Ferry, the Burnt Mills Ferry, and the Milford Ferry. The Milford Delaware Bridge Company built a three-span wooden covered bridge here in 1841–1842 at a cost of $27,000. Interestingly, when the 1903 flood destroyed the span nearest New Jersey, it was replaced with timbers that had washed down from the Riegelsville Bridge to the north, which was also destroyed by that flood. Like the Frenchtown and Stockton bridges, this bridge was also declared unfit for traffic in the 1930s. It was rebuilt in 1933 for a cost, including roadway approaches, of $89,970—in relative terms, not much more than its 1841 predecessor. The rebuilt bridge retains the camelback configuration, and its spans are of unequal length, ranging from 204 feet to 228 feet, for a total of 700 feet.

Still farther upriver is the Riverton-Belvidere Bridge, built in 1904 between Belvidere, the seat of government for Warren County since 1925, and Mount Bethel Township in Pennsylvania (see color plate 11). The first bridge at this site was a wooden covered bridge built between 1834 and 1836 by the Belvidere Delaware Bridge Company; four months after completion, most of the bridge was destroyed by high waters. Rebuilt between 1838 and 1839, it survived until the 1903 flood. The Delaware River Joint Toll Bridge Commission booklet notes that the nineteenth-century bridge was subject to a foreclosure action. Apparently, as of 1881, the bridge company had never paid a dividend. By act of the state legislature, whoever purchased the bridge was empowered to organize a new company with new stock.

The current four-span, riveted-steel Warren through-truss bridge is about 652 feet in length, with three of its spans just over 153 feet and the fourth nearly 170 feet. It cost approximately $25,000 to build in 1904, surprisingly less than the

$27,000 required to build the wooden Upper Black Eddy–Milford Bridge half a century earlier. In 1929 the Riverton-Belvidere Bridge was purchased by Pennsylvania and New Jersey for $60,000, and no more tolls were charged.

CENTRE (STOCKTON) BRIDGE

According to Stockton Borough's Web site, John Reading was among the proprietors of the colony of West Jersey who met with Native Americans in 1703 to purchase the land that ultimately became Stockton. The site of the ferry he founded there was part of the dowry his daughter brought to her marriage to Daniel Howell, and the operation became known as Howell's Ferry. In 1792 their son sold the property to John Prall Jr., who established the Prallsville Mill, which still stands and houses various art displays.

In 1811 the legislatures of New Jersey and Pennsylvania authorized a bridge to be built across the Delaware River to connect Stockton to Solebury Township, Pennsylvania. New Jersey required forty subscribers for four hundred shares of

CENTRE (STOCKTON) BRIDGE   This image shows the subdivided Warren truss, with vertical members intersecting the V's and inverted V's.

stock before the governor would issue "letters patent" for the construction. With the requisite investors, the Centre Bridge Company was founded. ("Centre" refers to the location of the bridge, between Trenton and Phillipsburg, where bridges had opened in 1806.) In 1812 the company hired Captain Peleg Kingsley and Benjamin Lord as construction supervisor and assistant, respectively, for the bridge's construction, and they brought it to completion in 1814. Like others in this era, it was a wooden covered bridge, here employing the Town lattice truss. The bridge was partly rebuilt in 1829 and repaired again after damage by floodwaters in 1841. With the arrival of a railroad here in mid-century, the name of the town became Centre Bridge Station.

Unlike the other wooden covered bridges from Phillipsburg to Trenton, this one survived the flood of 1903, only to be destroyed by a lightning-caused fire in 1923. The stone masonry piers and abutments remained, and were acquired in 1925 by the Joint Commission for Eliminating Toll Bridges, a venture of Pennsylvania and New Jersey. The commission built the current six-span Warren through-truss bridge in 1926–1927 on the existing foundations (which were encased in reinforced concrete). The bridge is approximately 864 feet long, with spans ranging from 100 feet to 152 feet in length. On the Pennsylvania side, the bridge also crosses the Pennsylvania Canal. Today, the successor to the Joint Commission, the Delaware River Joint Toll Bridge Commission, is responsible for this and other non-toll bridges across the Delaware.

LOWER TRENTON ("TRENTON MAKES") BRIDGE

The Lower Trenton Bridge may be to Trentonians what the Golden Gate Bridge is to San Franciscans: a symbol of their pride in their city, its history, and its citizens. Moreover, it stands on the site of one of the most significant bridges in early American history.

Before there was a bridge here, at the navigable head of the Delaware River, crossings to the Pennsylvania side were made by ferry. According to Lida Newberry, the first ferry was chartered in 1726 to James Trent, son of the city's namesake, William Trent. The first bridge, which opened in January 1806 (construction began in 1804), was a wooden covered bridge built at a cost of $180,000 at the time.

It stood on the same site as today's bridge. According to Eleanor Shuman, this first bridge at the state's capital city "was dedicated with elaborate ceremonies," and it was regarded as "one of the architectural wonders of the New World."

The writer of the first American book devoted to bridge construction, Thomas Pope, agreed. In *A Treatise on Bridge Architecture* (1811), he discussed important bridges in history, citing Julius Caesar's timber bridge and various bridges in Tibet, China, Italy, Switzerland, Africa, Norway, France, and England. The bridge at Trenton was one of fewer than a dozen American bridges he mentioned. A major reason for its significance was its builder, Theodore Burr, one of the preeminent and sought-after bridge builders of the day. Interestingly, Pope described Burr as the "architect" of the bridge. As mentioned in the introduction, the roles of architect and engineer would diverge over time. Burr's contribution to timber bridge construction was to improve the truss by adding an arc for support. Pope wrote that "this mode of constructing wooden arcs is considered as a great improvement in Bridge architecture . . . it is supposed to possess many advantages over those formed of solid and massy pieces of timber." He compared the strength of the Delaware River crossing to that of the bridge across the Hudson River at Waterford–Fort Miller and the one across the Connecticut River at Springfield, Massachusetts. The Trenton bridge, "we are assured by Mr. Burr, combines double the strength of either of them; but what constitutes the greatest excellence of the Delaware Bridge is the prospect of its durability."

LOWER TRENTON BRIDGE   More popularly known as the "Trenton Makes Bridge," this span is possibly the only bridge in the state that carries a slogan.

Burr's bridge was so highly regarded that it was pictured on the three-dollar notes issued by the Trenton Banking Company. In their *Historical Collections of the State of New Jersey* (1844) John W. Barbor and Henry Howe reproduced a woodcut that shows five arches that look like wedges of lemon, with the braces emanating from a center point of each span. A log roof covers the bridge, but the sides of each span are open. Wheaton J. Lane, in his study of New Jersey transportation, noted that "the Trenton bridge was a unique piece of engineering and travelers came from all points to inspect it." Surprisingly, however, "despite the high tolls charged, the Trenton Delaware Bridge gave only a moderate return to the stockholders."

Stagecoach traffic made regular use of the 1806 bridge. The first stagecoach to Trenton had operated since 1723, and regular service began in 1756. The stage wagon—a springless covered wagon—carried passengers and freight from Perth Amboy to Trenton, where the journey to Philadelphia was completed by boat. In 1772, the "Flying Machine," a wagon drawn by four horses and carried on springs, could make the journey from New York to Philadelphia in one and one-half days. The crossing between Trenton and Morrisville was made by ferry. Stagecoaches in those days had flamboyant names. Shuman cites some in *The Trenton Story*: "The Diligence," "The Industry," and "The Mail Pilot." It is hard today, perhaps, to imagine the scene as one of these made its way across the famous bridge.

The bridge was durable and high enough on its stone piers to survive the 1841 flood that destroyed other, newer bridges along the Delaware. In 1842 it was the first American bridge to carry an interstate railroad. By 1875, though, after being widened and moved slightly, the bridge was considered obsolete and taken down, replaced by other railroad and general traffic bridges. Within fifty years, the general traffic bridge could no longer serve the needs of the crossing, so the subdivided Warren truss bridge that now stands was built in 1928. Unlike many of the other truss bridges crossing the Delaware, this one has a camelback configuration, here a polygonal top chord with five slopes. The bridge is approximately 1,000 feet long, its five spans ranging in length from 166 feet (nearest the New Jersey side) to 206 feet and 210 feet (nearest the Pennsylvania side).

The sign "Trenton Makes, the World Takes" was placed on the bridge in 1935, reflecting the city's prominence then as an industrial center. During the first half of the eighteenth century, Trenton, as the midway point between New York and Philadelphia, was an important transportation hub. Shuman claims that Trenton led the iron and steel industry between 1847 and 1867, and refers to the first wrought-iron beams made by the Trenton Iron Works and John Roebling's steel cable plant. Roebling's factory buildings still stand. The ceramics industry also made important developments and flourished in Trenton in the nineteenth and early twentieth centuries.

The bridge that proclaims this fame is now often referred to as the "Trenton Makes Bridge." The Trenton Titans minor league hockey team proudly uses the bridge as its logo.

EASTON-PHILLIPSBURG TOLL BRIDGE

Just to the north of the Northampton Street Bridge in Phillipsburg (a toll-free cantilever bridge featured later in this book) stands the Depression-era Easton-Phillipsburg Toll Bridge, which cost $2.5 million to build. Dedicated on January 14, 1938, it was proclaimed "The World's Most Brilliant Bridge." It stands 52 feet (on average) above the level of the Delaware River, and its main span is 540 feet long.

EASTON-PHILLIPSBURG
TOLL BRIDGE   Today, a girder bridge would probably be built over
                       this kind of crossing.

The Pennsylvania (Petit) truss employed here was used from approximately 1875 to the early twentieth century. It is a variation on the Parker truss, with the addition of sub-struts and sub-ties, and generally spanned distances of approximately 250 to 600 feet. The Parker truss, in use from the mid-nineteenth to the twentieth century, was basically a Pratt truss with a polygonal top chord and covered distances of 40 to 200 feet. As can be seen, truss designs were often variations on the few basic types discussed earlier.

This toll bridge played a part in the controversial history surrounding U.S. Highway 22. In 1916 a group of "road boosters" organized the William Penn Highway Association of Pennsylvania to establish an alternative to the Lincoln Highway. In 1926 the American Association of State Highway Officials (AASHO) approved a numbering plan and routing for Route 22 that closely matched the proposed William Penn Highway. Pennsylvania objected, however, because the numbering plan affected roadways the state had already designated by name. By 1931, when the AASHO approved changes in Pennsylvania that altered the line of Route 22, a separate group, the Ben Franklin Highway Association, sought to increase the credibility of its route by obtaining U.S. road numbers. In 1938, when the Easton-Phillipsburg Toll Bridge opened, another shift in Route 22 occurred to a new approach east of Easton. Officially, Route 22 runs from Newark, New Jersey, to Cincinnati, Ohio, traversing this bridge.

BETSY ROSS BRIDGE

The Betsy Ross Bridge was built to connect Pennsauken, New Jersey, to Philadelphia. It provides an alternate crossing to the Tacony-Palmyra Bridge to the north and the Benjamin Franklin Bridge to the south. Because the Delaware River is a navigable waterway at this point, the bridge stands 135 feet over the mean high water. The bridge cost $103 million and required 29,326 tons of structural steel for itself and its approaches. The main span is 729 feet, and each of the two side spans is 364.5 feet. Writing in 1980, William Shank noted that the bridge's width of 105 feet, enough to accommodate eight lanes for traffic, gives it "one of the widest roadways of any bridge in the world."

Construction began in 1969. Although the bridge was completed in 1974, its opening was delayed by fears of neighborhood destruction in the Bridesburg sec-

·tion of Philadelphia, where the bridge is anchored on the Pennsylvania side. Opponents included Governor Milton Shapp of Pennsylvania and Mayor Frank L. Rizzo of Philadelphia. On opening day, April 30, 1976, New Jersey Governor Brendan Byrne faced about 150 demonstrators on the Pennsylvania side, who demanded barricades to protect Bridesburg. For a time, the bridge was considered a "white elephant" because it failed to attract drivers, who preferred the nearby Tacony-Palmyra Bridge. The Delaware River Port Authority had to resort to an advertising campaign to seek users.

The brochure for the opening of the bridge describes Betsy Ross as the person "generally credited with the fabrication of the first official flag of the United States" and as a woman who "conducted herself admirably through a long, difficult and eventful life." A role model in that Bicentennial year, "[s]he was brave and resourceful, a patriotic and loyal American; a talented and creative craftsperson and one of America's first 'liberated women.'" Her maiden name was Elizabeth Griscom, and in many ways she seemed ahead of her time. Born a Quaker, she was apprenticed to an upholsterer, whose work included flag making. She met and fell in love with fellow employee John Ross, an Episcopalian. Because interdenominational marriages were frowned upon and could result in communal isolation, she eloped with Ross and married him in New Jersey in November 1773, becoming estranged from her family. The Rosses began their own upholstery business in New

BETSY ROSS BRIDGE   An interesting feature of this Warren truss bridge is the way the truss descends below the level of the deck.

Jersey. Although the legend surrounding Betsy Ross's meeting with George Washington, which inspired her to design the first American flag, is subject to challenge, documentation in the minutes of the State Navy Board of Pennsylvania shows that she was commissioned to make the "colours" for Pennsylvania state ships. By the time she died in 1836, she had outlived by almost twenty years the last of her three husbands. So, regardless of the flag legend, Betsy Ross was a woman who faced down the conventions of her time to marry whom she chose and to support herself and her family by her intelligence and her skills. The Delaware River Port Authority claims that the Betsy Ross Bridge is "the first U.S. bridge named after a woman."

COVERED BRIDGES

Sometimes called "kissing bridges," because of their concealing features, covered bridges often have romantic connotations. However, the primary purpose of a cover over the deck and trusses of a wooden bridge was to shield them from snow and rain, and therefore decay and rot. Eric Sloan, in his classic *American Barns and Covered Bridges*, suggests several more reasons: to keep the roadway dry, to make the structure more solid, to give it a barnlike appearance (thereby making it more "animal-friendly"), and to prevent the bridge from drying out.

Most of America's covered bridges were constructed between 1825 and 1875. Multiple king-post trusses were often used. (Recall that the king-post truss is a triangle split down the middle by a vertical member to create two triangles.) In particular, the Howe truss, a modified king-post truss, was common in American covered bridge construction. Its metal vertical members are in tension, being pulled apart, while the wood diagonal members are in compression, being pushed together. It resembles a series of boxed Xs. A popular variation was the so-called Burr truss, which was basically a Howe truss with a curved (arch) wooden support along the panels for additional strength.

Among the oldest extant covered bridges are ones in Lucerne, Switzerland, that date from the fourteenth century. In the United States, there is some disagreement over the identification of the country's earliest covered bridge. Photographer and author David Plowden states that "[a]lthough covered bridges had been used extensively in Europe and an American design for one at Market Street, Philadelphia, had been published in 1787, the Permanent Bridge was the first to be constructed in the United States." That "Permanent Bridge" was completed in 1805 by master bridge builder Timothy Palmer (1751–1821) across the Schuylkill River.

On the other hand, Russell Roberts claims that the bridge built in 1772 at Raritan Landing, near New Brunswick, "was the first covered bridge in New Jersey." Norman Brydon agrees that "New Jersey's first covered bridge, and one of the earliest in the nation," was the three-span Raritan Landing Bridge. Yet, if it is only "one of the earliest," there must be others staking a claim. There is no dispute, however, as to when the idea was patented in the United States. Eric Sloan observes that the first U.S. patent for a covered bridge was issued to Charles W. Peale in 1797. As it happens, Palmer built his bridge on Peale's proposed site.

According to Norman Brydon, in *Of Time, Fire, and the River*, at any given time in New Jersey there were at most thirty-five covered bridges. Several of these, as noted in other sections of this book, were significant crossings over the Delaware River that were destroyed in whole or in part by the major floods of 1832, 1841, 1846, 1862, 1888, 1903 (the "Great Pumpkin Flood"), 1904, and 1955. Some of them were replaced by the metal truss bridges we see today.

Covered bridges were found in all but three of New Jersey's counties (Atlantic, Monmouth, and Morris). At present, only Green Sergeant's Bridge survives from the nineteenth century. The Scarborough Bridge over the North Branch of the Cooper River, dating from 1959, is the only other significant covered bridge in New Jersey.

GREEN SERGEANT'S BRIDGE

Sometimes referred to as the Sergeantsville Bridge, this eighty-four-foot-long structure across the Wickecheoke Creek in Delaware Township is the only surviving pre-1900 covered wooden truss bridge in New Jersey. It was originally built in 1866 as a queen-post truss but modified to be a Howe truss in 1872; steel stringers have since been installed to help with the live loads. Charles Ogden Holcombe built the bridge, with assistance in masonry work on the abutments provided by Ely and Charles Everitt, who were able to use the piers that had supported an earlier bridge

GREEN SERGEANT'S BRIDGE   New Jersey's sole remaining covered bridge
from the nineteenth century is a source of
local pride.

on the site from 1750. At present, there are really two bridges here. A second bridge
was built in 1961 to allow two-way traffic.

Ownership of the site can be traced back to Charles Sergeant in 1805. Upon his
death in 1833, title passed to his son, Richard Green Sergeant, for whom the bridge
was named. The town of Sergeantsville dates to 1827 and was once known as
Skunktown, allegedly because of the local trade in skunk pelts.

The only other significant covered bridge on public property in New Jersey is
the fifty-five-foot-long Scarborough Covered Bridge across the North Branch of the
Cooper River in Cherry Hill (see color plate 13). Built in 1959 by developer Robert
Scarborough, it was dedicated on Valentine's Day that year. The designer was
architect Malcolm Wells, who employed a lattice Town truss. Scarborough pur-
portedly sought to emulate the covered bridges in Bucks County, Pennsylvania,
although this bridge has an incomplete A frame and diagonal braces over the
pedestrian walkway.

Note, by the way, that those in the know pronounce the name of New Jersey's
historic covered bridge like the word "surgeon," not "sergeant"; that is, one says
"Green *Surgeonts*" or "*Surgeontsville*."

CANTILEVER BRIDGES

The cantilever bridge was a popular type in New Jersey in the first half of the twentieth century. In cantilever construction, the bridge can be built from both sides of the crossing simultaneously, either meeting or having a final center span put into place to link the two extended "diving board" spans. Another way to think of the cantilever is to imagine two airplanes touching wingtip to wingtip. Basically, instead of having the supports at either end of the span, the span is anchored at or toward one end, and the other, longer end overhangs.

The load distribution on a cantilever bridge—the dead load and the live load in the center—push down, creating compressive force. As they do so, they put pressure on the side cantilevered spans, creating tension, because there is a "pulling" force upward. There is also compressive force on the piers that sustain the cantilevered side spans. All of these forces need to balance each other and handle the live load forces that traverse the cantilever span to the main suspended span and then back to the other cantilever span.

Among the advantages of cantilever bridges are that they can span wide spaces and can be built without the need of expensive falseworks (used to support the bridge until it is completed, and then removed) or foundation piers, which can disrupt the flow of a river. Another advantage to the bridge is its rigidity, allowing rail transportation to be accommodated. These utilitarian qualities, however, can be offset by some aesthetic as well as practical considerations. One Web site devoted to bridges, www.brantacan.co.uk, observes that one "problem with appearance is that the cantilevers need to taper from the supports to the ends, whereas the suspended span needs to be narrow at the ends and thicker in the middle." The design also requires precision in alignment; because steel contracts and expands with the weather, the final placement of the suspended middle span must be coordinated with weather conditions.

Various sources trace the origin of the cantilever bridge to China as far back as the fourth century B.C.E. The wooden cantilever beam was known as the "flying bridge" or "extended arm bridge," and reached to approximately 20 meters. David Steinman wrote in *Bridges and Their Builders* that the Chinese built cantilever bridges for spans ranging from 30 to 130 feet, using wooden caissons filled with stone or rubble, into which the cantilever arms were driven. The central pier often featured a pagoda, house, or gateway, so that such bridges became the equivalent of the European or American town center.

The thirteenth-century French engineer Villard de Honnecourt drew a cantilever truss as a solution to spanning a waterway with a twenty-foot timber. As engineer Henry Petroski explored at length in *Invention by Design*, Galileo discussed the cantilever beam in his *Dialogues Concerning Two New Sciences* (1638) in the context of solids resisting fracture. He concluded that the beam's strength is proportional to the square of the depth of the beam.

The precursor of the modern cantilever bridge was the so-called Gerber Bridge, named for Bavarian engineer Heinrich Gerber, built in 1867 over the River Main at Hassfurt, Germany. On the American continent, one of the first appearances of a Gerber-type bridge was the railroad cantilever bridge built over Niagara Gorge in 1883 by Charles Conrad Schneider. Francis E. Griggs Jr. refers to this bridge as the first modern metal cantilever bridge in the United States, although other sources cite a bridge designed by Charles Smith across the Kentucky River at Harrodsburg, built in 1876–1877 for the Cincinnati Southern Railroad. The Niagara Gorge Bridge rose contemporaneously with one of the most famous early steel cantilever bridges, the Firth of Forth Bridge in Scotland. The relative newness of the form triggered popular interest. Petroski, in *Engineers of Dreams*, quotes the editor of *Engineering News* replying in 1887 to the question: "[W]hat is a Cantilever bridge?":

The term, as applied to a bridge, is of comparatively recent origin, but the principle is as old as the Hindoos and the art of building itself. It has been applied to wooden bridges for centuries, and it is only its later scientific solution by modern builders of steel and iron bridges that has brought it forward again prominently. Its advantage over other forms of truss construction is, that by a proper method of anchoring or balancing and the arrangement of its tension and compression members, it can be erected over space without supporting false-work.

Petroski further notes the interest in cantilever construction among American engineers from the last decades of the nineteenth century and into the twentieth. Cantilever principles were used in the construction of the famous steel arch Eads Bridge (1874) in St. Louis, Missouri, designed by James Buchanan Eads. Theodore Cooper, one of this country's principal engineers, used the cantilever design in building the Quebec Bridge over the St. Lawrence River in Quebec City, Canada, in the early years of the twentieth century. That bridge collapsed while under construction in 1907, when its compression members buckled owing to miscalculations as to the amount of steel needed to support the weight of the bridge, causing the steel beams to become deformed. The failure of this bridge because of such miscalculations reverberated throughout the world of engineering and led to a higher level of mathematical and scientific analysis in engineering applications. A second Quebec Bridge, another cantilever, was completed in 1917. In the meantime, concerns about safety influenced other cantilever designs, such as the Queensboro (59th Street) Bridge then under construction in New York. At the time it was completed in 1909, the Queensboro Bridge was the longest cantilever bridge in the United States.

More than any other type of steel bridge, cantilever bridges seem to this author to resemble the old Erector-set constructions. Others use different metaphors. In commenting on the Commodore John Barry Bridge (1974), Assemblyman Kenneth A. Gewertz of Gloucester County described it as being "wired together like a model airplane." The consulting architect on the Queensboro Bridge reportedly compared that bridge to a blacksmith's shop.

Cantilever principles may be applied to construction materials other than steel. Although the German engineer Ulrich Finsterwalder (1897–1988) was discussed in more detail in the introduction, it is worth recalling here that he conceived of the use of prestressed concrete in cantilever bridge construction. Examples are his Bendorf Bridge (1965) across the Rhine River at Koblenz, Germany, and the Mangfall Bridge (1960) near Munich.

Over the decades, improved engineering and technology have simplified the construction of cantilever bridges. David Steinman contrasted the four days of jacking needed in 1917 to get the center span in place on the Quebec Bridge with the thirty-five minutes required for the same operation in 1927 on the Carquinez Strait Bridge in California. By the 1920s, when the Goethals Bridge and Outerbridge Crossing were built, safety and economic issues seem to have been resolved favorably. However, with the advent of cable-stayed bridges, which can span comparable distances, cantilever construction may no longer be seen as advantageous. The opening to traffic of the Charles River cable-stayed bridge in Boston in 2003 may portend the future of bridge construction. Some observers even believe that the Commodore Barry Bridge will remain the longest cantilever bridge in the United States, because it is unlikely that such long cantilevers will again be constructed in this age of the cable-stayed bridge.

NORTHAMPTON STREET BRIDGE

The Northampton Street Bridge connects Phillipsburg, New Jersey, to Easton, Pennsylvania, across the Delaware River. This is one of the more distinctive-looking cantilever bridges in New Jersey because it does not have the caterpillar shape of the others featured in this book. At first glance, in fact, it looks like a suspension bridge.

A map from 1654 shows a Lenape Indian village, Chintewink, on the site of today's Phillipsburg. The name Phillipsburg first appears on a map published in 1749. Sources differ as to whether the city was named for a chief of the Lenape or one of the city's early landholders.

Ferry service began here in 1739, licensed by King George II to David Martin. Over the following decades, Martin leased the ferry to others, including Thomas Bullman, who bought the ferry privilege in 1798 and also established a tavern in Phillipsburg. Eventually, as happened elsewhere along the Delaware, the ferries here could no longer handle the volume of traffic, especially when the vicissitudes of weather and natural conditions, such as ice, impeded steady and dependable service. By 1795, the necessary authorization for building a bridge was granted by the legislatures of both Pennsylvania and New Jersey, and the Delaware Bridge Company, Inc., was formed. Construction began in 1797, but stalled for lack of funds. New Jersey and Pennsylvania authorized lotteries to raise funds and extended the time for completion. With fresh resources, the company retained Timothy Palmer, famed builder of the Permanent Bridge (1805) in Philadelphia. The three-span covered bridge he built in Phillipsburg was completed in 1806 and stood until the Northampton Street Bridge replaced it in 1895.

Palmer was a carpenter and self-taught engineer who had achieved renown in New England. The covered bridge at Phillipsburg was his last before he retired. Like many of the long covered bridges across the Delaware River, it had windows for light and for disposal of the manure that accumulated inside. About ten years before the bridge was demolished and replaced by the current one, rail tracks were laid across it.

Phillipsburg has long been a significant transportation center. In its early days, the settlement provided a link to the western frontier through its ferry service. Those ferries provided food and military supplies for George Washington's army,

NORTHAMPTON
STREET BRIDGE   The oldest of the cantilever bridges featured in this book, and perhaps the oldest significant one still standing in New Jersey, it resembles a suspension bridge. The renowned American photographer Walker Evans photographed it from the Easton side, very close to this view, during the 1930s.

which often camped in the northern part of the state. The area was also the terminal point of the Morris Canal, a major engineering feat completed in 1832.

Across the river, Easton is a significant educational and industrial center, as well as a point on the Lehigh Canal. The city's Centre Square (once known as the Great Square) was the site for one of the three readings of the Declaration of Independence on July 8, 1776, here delivered by Robert Levers from the steps of the courthouse.

The Northampton Street Bridge is also known as the "Free Bridge" in recognition of its purchase in 1921 by the Joint Commission for Eliminating Toll Bridges. Its main span is 300 feet, with two side spans running 125 feet each. It resembles a suspension bridge because of its eyebar design. The eyebar suspension system employs flattened rings to link the chains on suspension bridges. Steven Ostrow defines an eyebar as "a metal bar, generally rectangular in cross-section, enlarged at each end for holes, or 'eyes.'" In the case of the Northampton Street Bridge, the purpose of the eyebars is aesthetic rather than structural. According to the American Society of Civil Engineers (ASCE), the only other similarly designed bridges known to exist in the United States are the Frisco Bridge (1892) across the Mississippi in Memphis, Tennessee, and the swing span of the bridge across the Mississippi at Rock Island, Illinois (1893).

Charles Macdonald of the Union Bridge Company, who was president of the ASCE in 1893, built the Northampton Street Bridge. The engineer behind it was James Madison Porter III (1864–1928). He was the grandson of James Madison Porter, who served as secretary of war under President John Tyler for almost a year until the Senate rejected him. Undeterred, Porter went on to serve in the state legislature of Pennsylvania, and he became president of the Delaware, Lehigh, Schuylkill, and Susquehanna Railroad. Porter III was a graduate of Lafayette College, which his grandfather helped to found in 1826, and he taught civil engineering there following private practice with local firms, including a steel fabricating company.

A plaque on the Northampton Street Bridge records its history (though in some respects it disagrees with the dates provided by the Delaware River Joint Toll Bridge Commission):

> This structure replaces a covered wooden bridge of three spans, each about 155 feet clear, supported by two hollow piers, 35 feet by 55 feet and two abutments. Built by Timothy Palmer, 1805. At time of removal being next to the oldest, if not the oldest, wooden highway bridge in the United States.

Dimensions of Present Bridge

A cantilever bridge, 550 feet between end pins, two shore arms and two river arms, 125 feet each, suspended span, 50 feet, trusses, 38 feet 8 inches. Material, medium steel. Built 1885, by Union Bridge Co. Elevation of capstone on pier, 187.87 feet above mean tide, at Sandy Hook.

Easton-Phillipsburg Bridge

Rebuilt and Reopened October 23, 1957 following great flood of August 19, 1955.

GOETHALS BRIDGE

Ferries began to operate between Staten Island and Elizabeth (then Elizabethtown) in 1671. During Revolutionary times, a pontoon bridge spanned Howland Hook to Elizabeth. Following World War I, the increased construction and traffic needs in the region intensified the pressure for bridges to connect Staten Island to New Jersey and New York. The legislatures of both New York and New Jersey had been introducing such measures since 1868; finally, the idea was one whose time had come.

The Goethals Bridge was constructed between 1924 and 1928, at a cost of $7.2 million, between Elizabeth, New Jersey, and Howland Hook, Staten Island. Its main and two side spans total 1,824 feet, according to Steve Anderson (the Port Authority's Web site puts the truss span lengths at 1,152 feet and gives an overall length of 7,100 feet). Because the land at both ends of the span is low, a lengthy approach viaduct was needed (8,600 feet on 79 piers) to give the bridge room to rise. Consistent with the military requirement to maintain navigable waterways, the bridge clears the high-water mark by 135 feet. The 62-foot-wide bridge was originally conceived to carry trains as well as vehicles, but that design was changed for the final version. From time to time a plan comes forward to "twin" the bridge, but so far has been opposed by Staten Islanders fearful of increased traffic.

The Goethals Bridge carries vehicular, pedestrian, and bicycle traffic across Arthur Kill. Steve Anderson, in his Web site précis of the bridge, writes that a low-level bridge was originally considered to span this shallow channel. The New Jer-

sey State Board of Commerce favored a higher bridge, however, as more support-
ive of the state's ports. Similar opposition from shipping interests was overcome by
War Department approval of the 135-foot clearance. The legislatures of New York
and New Jersey delegated the project to the recently created Port Authority.
Regarding the reason this and the Outerbridge were the Authority's first projects,
Anderson quotes the then general counsel, Julius Cohen: "We wanted to begin
with something where we were most likely to succeed, and the smaller enterprise
was the better one for the purpose. If we succeeded, the George Washington
Bridge would come later. And so it did."

Originally expected to be called the Arthur Kill Bridge, after the waterway, the
bridge was renamed before its dedication to honor Major General George Washington Goethals, builder of the Panama Canal, who died just before the ceremony.
Handpicked by President Theodore Roosevelt from the Army Engineer Corps,
Goethals was able to complete the canal after years of failed efforts by others.
Goethals was also New Jersey's first state highway engineer and the first consulting engineer to the Port Authority. Appointed to the New Jersey position in 1917,
he resigned to become manager of the Emergency Fleet Corporation after the
United States entered World War I. He founded the engineering firm of George W.

GOETHALS BRIDGE   The truss arrangements make this bridge resemble a
caterpillar.

Goethals and Company in March 1919 and headed the firm until it dissolved in 1923, at which time he practiced alone in New York.

Renowned engineer Othmar Ammann had submitted plans to the Port Authority for construction of both of the bridges proposed to cross from Staten Island to New Jersey, but he lost out to J.A.L. Waddell, one of the more senior engineers of the time and famous for the Waddell A truss design, which he patented in 1894. The rationale advanced was that the new Port Authority needed someone of stature and recognition. The funds to pay for the Goethals and the Outerbridge were to be raised by bonds backed by the money-making ability of the bridges, so a highly reputable engineer was key to the project. Henry Petroski notes that the choosing of an engineer by competitive bidding was criticized by some as comparable to the selection of counsel to defend a lawsuit by taking the lowest bid. Interestingly, the Hardesty and Hanover Web site claims that it was Shortridge Hardesty, Waddell's protégé and partner, who designed the Goethals and Outerbridge crossings.

Nonetheless, the scope of the project exceeded the capabilities of a single engineer. Also involved besides Goethals was William Burr, a professor at Columbia University's School of Engineering and another notable engineer of the day. Ironically, or perhaps as proof of the small circle of engineers qualified to work on such projects, Ammann was appointed bridge engineer for the Port Authority in 1925 and so was later involved with the bridge in that capacity. He did not design it, however, as is sometimes mistakenly reported. Darl Rastorfer makes it clear that Ammann supervised the construction in his Port Authority role.

In *The Architecture of Bridges*, Elizabeth Mock described the Goethals Bridge as having "internal confusion . . . typical of an overhead truss with an uneven upper edge." Waddell himself is reported to have conceded some aesthetic failure, claiming that American engineers lacked architectural training, which he felt accounted for the ugliness of American steel bridges.

Although some observers may not consider it the most elegant of constructions, the Goethals Bridge should not be underestimated in terms of importance and achievement. There remains something impressive about the steel blue Goethals Bridge, clearly visible from the New Jersey Turnpike. It stands as a monument to its namesake and a vindication of the vision of the new Port Authority. In the right light, its distinctive sculptural engineering stands out in the industrial landscape, and this author finds it a particularly attractive element rising above the clutter of trains, weeds, pavement, wires, and factories.

1 DELAWARE RIVER VIADUCT Seen from the south, looking north, this beautiful arch bridge blends into the environment of the Delaware Water Gap.

2 OPEN BASCULE BRIDGE

According to the Environmental Protection Agency, this railroad bridge north of the Clay Street Bridge in the portion of the Passaic River known as the Kearny Reach was built by the Erie and Lackawanna Railroad. Gerald Oliveto identifies it as the "NX" Bridge, owned by the Norfolk Southern Railroad along the Newark Industrial Track.

3 NEWARK BAY BRIDGE
WITH RAILROAD BRIDGE   Seen from Route 440 in Bayonne, the
industrial area of Newark Bay is transformed
into an artistic composition.

4 ROEBLING FACTORY
SUSPENSION BRIDGE   This view shows not only the suspension bridge
but also a part of the Roebling factory in Trenton,
today used as various private and governmental
office buildings.

5 PORTLAND-COLUMBIA
PEDESTRIAN BRIDGE   This is one of only two exclusively pedestrian
bridges crossing the Delaware River.

6 READING RAILROAD
(WEST TRENTON) BRIDGE   As viewed from the Pennsylvania side of
the Delaware River, this bridge remains a
testament to the aesthetic appeal of the
great stone arch railroad bridges. The piers
of a prior bridge at this site are still visible
through the arches.

7 UPPER BLACK EDDY–
MILFORD BRIDGE

The camelback truss
is a feature this bridge
shares with the Lower
Trenton Bridge.

8 DELAWARE RIVER–
TURNPIKE TOLL BRIDGE   Built between 1954 and 1956, this steel-arch
bridge has a main span of 682 feet.

9 NEWARK
(PASSAIC RIVER) BRIDGES   In this view looking north, we see, first, the Bridge Street Bridge (a swing bridge), then the Newark Drawbridge (a railroad center-bearing swing bridge), and finally the almost Gothic William J. Stickel Memorial Bridge (a lift bridge).

10 OUTERBRIDGE CROSSING
WITH GREAT BEDS LIGHTHOUSE   This view was taken near Morgan Beach.

11 RIVERTON-
BELVIDERE BRIDGE   Like many bridges on the Delaware River, this one
was built after the flood of 1903 destroyed the
nineteenth-century wooden truss bridge at this site.

12 DELAWARE WATER GAP
TOLL BRIDGE   Notice the aesthetically pleasing round piers
sustaining this girder bridge across the Delaware
River in the vicinity of the Delaware Water Gap.

13 SCARBOROUGH
COVERED BRIDGE   Although relatively small and built in the mid-twentieth
century, this bridge captures the spirit of the
nineteenth century's covered bridges.

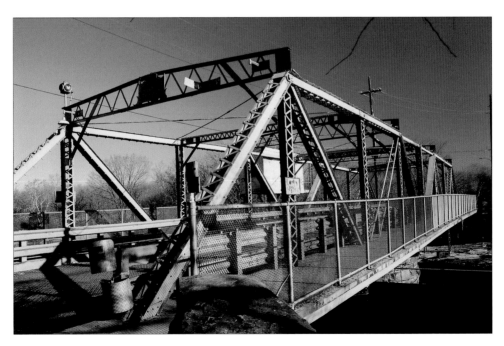

14 STATE STREET BRIDGE   This view of the swing bridge over the Cooper
River in Camden shows the shanty operator's
house.

15 EDISON BRIDGE   A second girder bridge, the Ellis Vieser Bridge, was constructed next to the original Edison Bridge and today carries the southbound lanes. The Edison Bridge is the nearer one in this view.

16 VICTORY BRIDGE   Although this bridge will be replaced soon, it is included here as a historically significant and impressive bridge over an important river in the state. Built in 1926 over the Raritan River, this swing span contains a tender's house, from which the rack-and-pinion drive is controlled. The new Victory Bridge will have a higher clearance than was feasible at this site in the first part of the twentieth century.

OUTERBRIDGE CROSSING

Constructed between 1924 and 1928, the Outerbridge Crossing is often assumed to have taken its name from its location. Because it is located farther from New York City than its companion to the north, the Goethals Bridge, people assume it is an "outer" bridge. However, this bridge was named for Eugenius Harvey Outerbridge (1860–1932), an engineer and the first chairman of the then newly created Port Authority of New York and New Jersey.

Outerbridge, born in Philadelphia, had a varied career. He worked with the merchant firm of Harvey and Company in Newfoundland in the mid-1870s, and in 1878 moved to New York to serve as agent for the company. He founded his own import-export firm, Harvey and Outerbridge, in 1881, later ran the Pantasote Leather Company, and set up the Agasote Millboard Company in 1909, which in 1936 became the Homasote Company. His sister Mary was a leader in establishing tennis as a sport in the United States, and Outerbridge himself was involved with the founding of the U.S. Tennis Association. He was also active in various non-governmental agencies, headed the Chamber of Commerce of the State of New

OUTERBRIDGE CROSSING   It is hard to imagine this environment without the bridge. This view is from the south on the Staten Island side; see color plate 10 for a view from the New Jersey shoreline, showing the Great Beds Lighthouse.

York, and figured as a leader in the push for a port authority similar to those in Europe.

In an Internet commentary, his great-grandson quoted Outerbridge's description of the need for a coordinated transportation network within the area overseen by the Port Authority of New York and New Jersey:

> With 105 municipalities, with 12 trunk line railroads bringing in and taking out of or through the Port over 75,000,000 tons of freight per annum, with an immense number of foreign and domestic steamships, . . . an incalculable amount of local water-borne traffic, . . . 8,000,000 people within the district to be housed, clothed, fed, provided with the means of carrying on their business . . . , the whole problem might well be likened to a maze from which it is most difficult even for those with the most experience, with the most intensive study and with the application of the best judgement, to find the right way out.

Like the Goethals Bridge, this one was designed by J.A.L. Waddell, and Othmar Ammann supervised its construction. It cost $9.6 million and stands 135 feet over mean high water at mid-span. The Outerbridge Crossing is somewhat longer than its neighbor: its main and side spans total 2,850 feet, connecting Perth Amboy, New Jersey, across the Arthur Kill to Tottenville, Staten Island. (Again, this length, supplied by Steve Anderson, exceeds the Port Authority's stated length of 2,100 feet for the truss spans. Both sources note a total length of 8,800 feet, including the approaches.)

One footnote to the bridge: Its home, Perth Amboy, was one of the two capitals of provincial New Jersey. Here the last royal governor of the colony, William Franklin, the Loyalist son of Benjamin Franklin, was arrested in his home on Kearny Avenue on June 17, 1776, by American forces.

PULASKI SKYWAY

When people from out of state think of New Jersey, they invariably conjure up images of an industrial wasteland criss-crossed by the New Jersey Turnpike, with factories and oil refineries belching smoke into the air. Cutting through the core of this area defined by Elizabeth, Newark, Jersey City, and Secaucus is the Pulaski Skyway. Apart from its engineering significance, this bridge remains one of the most spectacular and graceful structures in the United States.

Depending upon who does the measuring and what terminal points are chosen, the length of this elevated viaduct, which crosses the Hackensack and Passaic rivers and connects Newark and Jersey City across the swampy Meadowlands, is said to be 6.2 miles (Eric DeLony), 3.6 miles (Lida Newberry), or 3.5 miles (John Cunningham). Steve Anderson observes that the bridge has two main 550-foot cantilever spans with through trusses, and four 350-foot side cantilever spans with deck trusses. Like the Goethals Bridge and Outerbridge Crossing, it clears the water with an elevation of at least 135 feet to accommodate War (now Defense) Department regulations; but at its highest point over the Hackensack River, it rises some 200 feet. In the other direction, Frank A. Reddan noted, excavations for the foundations for the piers sank to 147 feet below high-water level. He added that "the arch spans carry the roadway between the towers and give the effect of lightness combined with strength."

The designer, Sigvald Johannesson, used techniques similar to those employed on the Crown Point Bridge across Lake Champlain. Johannesson was a charter

PULASKI SKYWAY,
PASSAIC RIVER   The portion shown here is a through truss that carries
                   traffic over the Passaic River; the approach spans are
                   deck trusses.

member of the Mercer County chapter of the New Jersey Society of Professional Engineers and a former railroad engineer (he died in Trenton in April 1953). The politics of credit infuse this story, however. The *New York Times* reported in 1933 that the bridge was "designed under the direction of Jacob L. Bauer, State Highway Engineer," with no mention of Johannesson. Others who worked on the bridge include Harry Albert Balken, an engineer who assisted in designing and building the Chesapeake Bay Bridge (1952), the San Francisco–Oakland Bay Bridge (1936), and the Henry Hudson Bridge (1936); an engineer named H. W. Hudson; and another former railroad engineer, Frederick Lavis. David S. Fine, a noted engineer whose works include the arch of the Bayonne Bridge, also participated. As construction manager for the New York district of U.S. Steel, Fine supervised the hingeless arch of the Henry Hudson Bridge, the Bronx-Whitestone Bridge (1939), and the Tappan Zee Bridge (1955), as well as the spinning cables for the Triborough Bridge (1936).

Cunningham records that construction began on the Pulaski Skyway in 1930 and was completed in 1932 at a cost of $20–21 million. The bridge used 88,461

PULASKI SKYWAY, HACKENSACK RIVER   This is one of the most beautiful bridges in the state, if not the country, although driving it is for the quick-witted and alert.

tons of structural steel. Notably, the Kahnawake Mohawks, experienced steel-workers from the St. Lawrence region of Canada, worked on the bridge. Fifteen fatal accidents occurred during construction. (This number apparently does not include the murder that resulted from a labor dispute over union wages, which led Jersey City mayor Frank "Boss" Hague to send in the police to end a strike holding up construction.)

Fatalities on large bridge construction projects were not uncommon. David McCullough, in his account of the Brooklyn Bridge, accepts contemporary records that put the number of deaths at twenty during that monumental effort. Three workers were killed during construction of the Edison Bridge (1940; see color plate 15) across the Raritan River. In Roman times, too, the connection between rivers and death was real, because of the perceived need to placate the river gods at the start of a bridge project. Early Romans made annual human sacrifices to the Tiber River, but eventually substituted reed dummies in the ceremony. David Steinman refers to an old practice in Germany of throwing effigies into the river, and notes that "[e]ven in our own time, vestiges of this remain, when workers on a modern structure declare that 'the bridge demands a life.'"

The Pulaski Skyway opened on November 24, 1932. Its completion was called "the outstanding highway engineering achievement in history," according to John Cunningham. Frank Reddan recorded similar sentiments expressed by the chief of the Federal Bureau of Roads, who called it "the greatest highway project in the United States." The American Institute of Steel Construction named it "Most Beautiful Steel Structure" for 1932 in the Class A category for structures costing over $1 million. The bridge was built under the auspices of the New Jersey State Highway Department to accommodate the rail and truck traffic that began to clog the area as a result of troop movements in World War I. It also feeds traffic to the Holland Tunnel (built in 1927) and now carries approximately 60,000 vehicles daily.

Originally called the Diagonal Highway and then the Newark–Jersey City Viaduct, the bridge was renamed in May 1933 in honor of the Polish-born patriot Casimir Pulaski, who served with George Washington and died during the American struggle for independence. Listeners to Orson Welles's original "War of the Worlds" broadcast on October 30, 1938, would have heard that the skyway had been destroyed by Martians. The area over which the skyway passes is also famous for one of the garbage dumps, Moscato's, where labor leader James Hoffa is rumored to be buried.

COMMODORE JOHN BARRY BRIDGE

The Commodore John Barry Bridge, built from 1969 to 1974 across the Delaware River between Bridgeport, New Jersey, and Chester, Pennsylvania, is among the longest cantilever spans in the world. The qualification is important, because varying sources disagree about its world ranking. In 1997 Judith Dupré listed it as the fourth longest cantilever bridge in the world, with a main span of 1,622 feet; in her ranking, it is just ahead of the two Greater New Orleans Bridges and is thus the longest in the United States. On the other hand, a 1984 article in *Engineering News Record* contends that, although the Commodore Barry Bridge is longer than the two New Orleans bridges, they have the longest actual cantilevers in the United States. William Shank adds a further qualification: the bridge is "said to be

COMMODORE
JOHN BARRY BRIDGE   A small park at the foot of the bridge affords this view looking east toward New Jersey. The complex truss arrangement that is clearly visible here is sometimes criticized as cluttered.

the longest such cantilever main span of welded construction in the United States." It is perhaps not surprising that, apart from the cantilever portion of the San Francisco–Oakland Bridge, the other longest American cantilevers are all in Louisiana—at Gramercy and Baton Rouge—where marshy areas like the Meadowlands in New Jersey require long spans like the Pulaski Skyway.

As was the case at the sites of many Delaware River bridges, a ferry operator served the Chester-Bridgeport crossing as far back as the late eighteenth century. At one point, more than a million passengers per year used the ferries here, although numbers began to decline in 1971. The ferry service ended the day the bridge opened, on February 1, 1974.

Although the Delaware Memorial Bridge alleviated some of the transportation demands of southern New Jersey in the 1950s, there remained a thirty-mile gap between that bridge and the Benjamin Franklin and Walt Whitman bridges connecting Philadelphia and Camden to the north. The primary purpose of the Commodore John Barry Bridge was to facilitate the economic development of the Chester-Bridgeport area. However, twenty years after completion of the bridge, an article in the *Philadelphia Inquirer* concluded that it had encouraged only limited economic progress in the region.

Structurally, the main section is cantilever, with deck truss approaches. The two towers have caisson foundations and rise 418 feet above mean high water. To permit marine traffic, the mid-span clearance is 192 feet, significantly higher than the 135 feet required for navigation when the Goethals Bridge and Outerbridge Crossing were built in northern New Jersey. Forty-nine thousand tons of structural steel went into the bridge and its approaches. The deck itself is eight inches thick and made of reinforced concrete. The cost of the original structure was $115 million. The firm of E. Lionel Pavlo provided engineering expertise on the project. That firm also designed the approaches to the Throgs Neck Bridge in New York (1961) and the substructure of the cantilever Greater New Orleans Bridges noted above, among other projects.

The Commodore John Barry Bridge is currently owned and operated by the Delaware River Port Authority. The bridge was named for the American Revolutionary war hero instrumental in founding the American navy.

SUSPENSION BRIDGES

In the prototypical suspension bridge, the deck is suspended by cables made of rope, steel, or some other material, which themselves are draped over towers and anchored at either end of the crossing. Modern suspension bridges have the anchored cables carried over large supporting towers, with a separate set of cables or wires holding up the deck below. Because it does not need intermediate piers to support the deck, the suspension bridge has been useful for spanning areas that need length as well as height clearance.

In India, according to David Brown, one can still find primitive suspension bridges, constructed of twisted bamboo rope, at lengths up to about 660 feet. Users traverse them by riding in a hoop. Variations on this primitive mechanism, also found in China, include a version where riders pull themselves along in a basket by hauling on another cable. Suspension bridges were known very early in China; these were built from bamboo until the end of the sixth century C.E., at which time wrought-iron cables took over, although it is possible that wrought iron was used as early as the first century C.E.

The Renaissance philosopher-scientist Faustus Verantius (1551–1617) described three suspension bridge designs in his *Machinae Novae*, published around 1615. These included a type of basket ropeway, a military bridge with ropes and deck, and an iron suspension bridge with eyebar tie rods—his "pons unius funis." Even earlier, in 1411, an aerial ropeway was illustrated in a book published in Vienna by Johannes Harddear. In Danzig in 1644, Adam Wybel built a suspension ropeway for carrying military supplies.

David Plowden identifies an iron chain bridge built in 1734 over the Oder River at Glorywitz, Prussia, as the earliest true suspension bridge in western Europe. It was built by the army of the Palatinate of Saxony. Perhaps the most significant early suspension bridge was the Menai Bridge, built in 1826 by Thomas Telford in Great Britain; it became the prototype for the modern suspension bridge, according to Stephen Johnson and Robert T. Leon. In 1834 suspension bridges took another leap forward with the construction of the Grand Pont Suspendu in Fribourg, Switzerland, by Joseph Chaley. Its span of 896 feet was the longest in the world and used cables made from a thousand wires in twenty strands. By employing trussed railings, it avoided the problem of oscillation. Ultimately, in 1923, it was replaced by a multi-span concrete bridge.

Plowden notes that the first American metal suspension bridge was built in 1801 by James Finley in Pennsylvania, and the nation's first wire suspension bridge was also built in that state, in 1816, by Josiah White and Erskine Hazard over the Schuylkill River. Finley's was also the first suspension bridge with a rigid, level deck for vehicles. William Shank describes the colorful Finley as a political figure who at different times was a justice of the peace, county commissioner, state representative, judge, successful lawyer, and inventor and engineer. He not only constructed at least thirteen bridges, but also held a patent on a suspension system, although his first patent was obtained in 1808, approximately seven years after the construction of his first bridge. Finley was followed by John Roebling (1806–1869) and Charles O. Ellet Jr. (1810–1862). Ellet designed the Wheeling Suspension Bridge over the Ohio River, built between 1847 and 1849.

The first suspension bridge for railroads was John Roebling's across the Niagara Gorge, built from 1851 to 1855. This massive structure, one of the few suspension bridges used for railroads, was replaced in 1897 by a steel arch bridge. According to David Brown, Roebling commented that he felt "less vibration" inside a train crossing his bridge than he did in his "brick dwelling at Trenton, N.J., during the rapid transit of an express train over the New Jersey R.R.," which passed within two hundred feet of his door. Roebling's factory in Trenton contributed cable wire to numerous bridges. A suspension bridge that linked two of the buildings of the plant still survives (see color plate 4). Although Roebling is best remembered for the the Brooklyn Bridge, completed in 1883, he built many other bridges, including the Delaware Aqueduct, now regarded as the oldest existing wire suspension bridge in the United States. Built in 1849 to carry the Delaware and Hudson Canal between Lackawaxen, Pennsylvania, and the New York side of the Delaware River, it is now used by vehicular traffic.

One of the most difficult and dangerous aspects of building a suspension bridge is the laying of caissons or cofferdams, which are used to construct the foundations for the towers. Cofferdams are built in place, whereas caissons are generally constructed elsewhere and moved into position. Lives were lost during construction of the George Washington Bridge when one of the cofferdams collapsed. Many workers on the Brooklyn Bridge suffered from "caisson disease" or, more descriptively, "the bends," from working in compression chambers underwater. It would be many years before medical science caught up with the engineering of such bridges.

Among the many steel suspension bridges constructed in the United States by the turn of the twentieth century, some of the most significant ones are in New Jersey. I am aware of eleven suspension bridges still existing in the state. In addition to the six featured in this section and the one that connects the buildings of the Roebling plant, there is a small Roebling suspension bridge in Mahlon Stacey Park in Trenton that is supposedly a small model of the Brooklyn Bridge. A pedestrian suspension bridge at Cranberry Lake in Sussex County leads to the Cranberry Lake Country Club. Finally, David Denenberg, in his comprehensive inventory of suspension bridges, includes two more pedestrian bridges: the Ravine Bridge ("Old Bouncer"; 1927) on the Douglass College campus of Rutgers University, and the Pochuck Quagmire Bridge (1994) on the Appalachian Trail in Vernon Valley.

RIEGELSVILLE BRIDGE

The bridge built by John A. Roebling's Sons Company in 1904 across the Delaware River to connect Riegelsville (Pohatcong Township), New Jersey, to Riegelsville (Durham Township), Pennsylvania, involved the designer of Phillipsburg's cantilever Northampton Bridge, Professor James Madison Porter III. The wooden covered bridge built at this site in 1835 (or 1837, according to Hunterdon County's Web site) by Porter's grandfather and Solon Chapin had been destroyed in the flood of 1903. Porter prepared an evaluation for the Riegelsville Delaware Bridge

Company that disagreed with a report supplied to the Roebling company as to the adequacy of the new bridge design. As a result, two additional 1¾-inch cables were added to the two planned 2⅝-inch cables. It is interesting that the venerable company founded by John Roebling would be second-guessed on matters of safety. The Brooklyn Bridge, designed by John Roebling and his son Washington, drew lessons from other bridge failures and in many ways overcompensated (if that is even possible) for stress.

Ferries served the crossing here until the wooden bridge opened. The name of the most famous of the ferry families is spelled variously Shank (according to Norman Brydon) and Shenk (according to Frank Dale). Eventually Benjamin Riegel bought the ferry around 1806 and became the namesake for the town.

The 577-foot Riegelsville Bridge is interesting from a structural and design perspective. In addition to the extra cables, it has wrought-iron eyebars embedded in concrete anchorages. The cables pass over cast-iron saddles on the towers. Stiffening trusses are connected to the floor and provide the sidewalk railings. At least one source (David Denenberg) claims that this bridge "is one of the few (if not the only)

RIEGELSVILLE BRIDGE   This elegant Roebling bridge is distinguished by relatively low towers, low-strung cables, and a rather high water clearance.

remaining American multi-span highway suspension bridge with continuous cables." Tolls were charged here until 1923, when the bridge was purchased by the Joint Commission for Eliminating Tolls. By the time this book is in print, the Riegelsville Bridge is expected to be added to the National Register of Historic Places.

Solon Chapin was responsible for the first bridge built on the site of the present-day Lumberville Pedestrian Bridge. The current bridge (discussed below) is also a suspension bridge built by John A. Roebling's Sons Company.

BENJAMIN FRANKLIN BRIDGE

From the time it opened on July 1, 1926, and for three years thereafter, the Benjamin Franklin Bridge held the title of longest suspension bridge in the world, with a center span of 1,750 feet between its two towers and two side spans of 872 feet. It was the age of the great suspension bridges. Just one year later, work would begin on the George Washington Bridge at the other end of New Jersey.

Construction on this first bridge between Camden, New Jersey, and Philadelphia had begun in 1922. Henry Petroski notes that the ground-breaking ceremony was somewhat unusual. Instead of some dignitary driving a shovel into the earth, a plank was torn from a pier that would be replaced by the bridge. At the ceremonies that opened the completed bridge, New Jersey Governor A. Harry Moore began his remarks by quoting the hymn "Blessed Be the Tie That Binds." President Calvin Coolidge came to the dedication ceremony a few days later. According to Walter Andariese's account, Coolidge dug a few spadefuls of dirt to cover the roots of a Vermont maple planted at the bridge and then remarked, "This is the kind of work I like."

Originally and officially known at its opening as the Delaware River Bridge, the span was also called the Camden-Philadelphia Bridge, or simply the Camden Bridge. According to the Delaware River Port Authority Web site, the Delaware River Joint Bridge Commission rejected the name "Franklin Bridge" in 1923. However, the bridge received that name officially in 1955, after a committee was appointed to name both it and the Walt Whitman Bridge, then under construction. It is now popularly known as the Ben Franklin.

Proposals for a bridge between Camden and Philadelphia date back to at least 1818, when two men from Camden suggested a 2,200-foot bridge from Camden to a mile-long island near Philadelphia; a ferry from the island to Philadelphia would finish the journey. That bridge was never built, nor was the four-span suspension bridge suggested in 1851 or Thomas Say Speakman's "double draw" suspension bridge proposed in 1868. Consequently, ferries continued to ply their trade here. To accommodate ever larger ferries, the island between Camden and Philadelphia was dredged away in the 1890s. Eventually, however, the growing population and industrial centers on the two sides of the river created sufficient political will for a bridge to be approved.

In 1919 the legislatures of Pennsylvania and New Jersey created the Delaware River Bridge Joint Commission. The enabling legislation specified that the states would share equally in the construction costs, but bear the costs of land acquisition within their jurisdictions individually. New Jersey bonded its share, and Pennsylvania paid half from state funds and half from Philadelphia funds.

A report by J.A.L. Waddell's firm, Waddell and Son, recommended a suspension bridge between Vine and Race streets in Philadelphia to Linden Street in Camden. A cantilever bridge at the site was rejected because such a bridge would have involved more steel, more expense, and more difficulty in financing. According to Andariese, one contractor dominated the market for cantilever construction, and

BENJAMIN FRANKLIN BRIDGE   The truss deck, unique towers, and massive anchors are visible in this view of the Philadelphia side of the bridge.

payments could not have been spread out over as much time as those for a suspension bridge. He adds that, aesthetically, the "slender towers" of a suspension bridge and the "graceful curves" of its cables were preferable to the "excessive network of criss-crossing girders" of a cantilever.

The chief engineer for the project was Ralph Modjeski, who also recommended the wire-cable suspension design over proposals for a cantilever or an eyebar suspension bridge. The plan incorporated "deflection theory," which Modjeski had used in his design for the Manhattan Bridge (1909). This theory is based on the assumption that a suspension bridge, as a result of its own weight and the downward force of traffic, creates its own stability without the need for expensive stiffening trusses on the deck. Consequently, the deck can be lighter to minimize strain on the cables. As summed up by David Billington in an interview, deflection theory considered the overall ability of the deck and cables to absorb the forces acting on the bridge, rather than analyzing the strengths of each of these elements in isolation. John Roebling had advocated the reverse: heavier structures are more stable.

Some sources credit the Viennese engineer Joseph Melan with originating deflection theory. Others cite the work of Leon S. Moisseiff, a mathematician who was involved in the design of the Manhattan Bridge, consulted on the George Washington and Bronx-Whitestone bridges, and served as Modjeski's design engineer on the Camden-Philadelphia project. Moisseiff later designed the Tacoma Narrows Suspension Bridge, which collapsed in 1940, the very year in which it was completed. One reason for the failure of that bridge, Darl Rastorfer notes, was that "Moisseiff's application of the deflection theory had unwittingly led to a road deck configuration with aerodynamic qualities somewhat like the wing of an airplane," causing instability in certain wind speeds.

Fortunately, and notwithstanding Modjeski's adoption of deflection theory, deep stiffening trusses were used over the main roadway deck in the Ben Franklin Bridge. Two cables of wire, each thirty inches in diameter, were also used, with their wires running parallel, not twisted around each other. The cables were designed by Holton D. Robinson, who also assisted in designing the Manhattan Bridge and the Williamsburg Bridge (1903).

Among the more distinctive features of the Ben Franklin are the two massive anchorages, each of which occupies three-quarters of an acre. They bear the respective seals of the cities and states in which they sit. For lack of the bedrock that supports the George Washington Bridge, the anchors had to be built primarily from concrete. Their primary purpose is to hold the pull of the cables and therefore sustain the towers, but they also support the elevated steel viaduct approaches to the main span. Architect Paul Philippe Cret designed the plazas at the end of the bridge and also, with Modjeski, the anchors. (This collaboration again reflects the synergy between the architectural and engineering professions in bridge building.) Cret also designated the color scheme for the bridge—gray with green trim. Eventually, however, the gray outlasted the green, and the bridge's superintendent in 1964, Frank Suplee, directed that it be painted completely gray, because that particular paint offered better protection for the bridge.

Although it was the longest suspension bridge in the world when it opened, at 3,536 feet (anchorage to anchorage), the Ben Franklin was not that much longer than the Brooklyn Bridge (3,455 feet), and was shorter than the Quebec cantilever bridge over the St. Lawrence River. Andariese, in his history of the Ben Franklin, notes that in 1976 there were twenty-eight suspension bridges in the United States with center spans in excess of 1,000 feet, yet there was no uniformity of tower design. He contends that the Ben Franklin's towers, now more than seventy-five years old, "have modern lines" and, although "just a bit ornate, are not really so obvious," conveying "an image of enduring strength rather than obsolescence." Gustav Lindenthal and others at the time criticized the design of the towers for appearing too utilitarian, but steel towers were cheaper than stone and involved less time in setting the foundations.

When traveling across the larger bridges like this one, we should remember that they are also memorials to the individuals who died in creating them. In all, fifteen men died while constructing the Ben Franklin Bridge, including a painter who fell to his death within a month after the bridge opened. It is also fitting to remember, in view of Gay Talese's appreciation of the contributions of Native Americans to bridge building in general, that one of the fatalities on the Ben Franklin was an Iroquois, Louis Rice, who was standing on a beam that came loose and fell.

The Ben Franklin Bridge is owned and managed by the Delaware River Port Authority, which was originally established in 1919 as the Delaware River Bridge Joint Commission. The federal legislation that created the authority in 1951, following an agreement between Pennsylvania and New Jersey, entrusted the agency with the mission of promoting international trade along the Delaware. A second bill authorized construction of what is now the Walt Whitman Bridge.

When the Ben Franklin Bridge opened, tolls ranged from a high of seventy-five cents for certain trucks to ten cents for a motorcycle or bicycle. It was free to pedestrians, but a horse and rider had to pay fifteen cents; a horse or mule on a lead, along with cows, hogs, and sheep, was subject to a charge of twenty cents.

GEORGE WASHINGTON BRIDGE

It might fairly be said that the George Washington Bridge is to New Jersey and New York what the Golden Gate Bridge is to California. It is a work of art, its exposed towers distinctive and beautiful. The original design called for them to be encased in masonry and concrete, like those of the Brooklyn Bridge, but that plan was abandoned at the onset of the Great Depression. To see this bridge at night, looking either north up the Hudson River or to the west when traveling southbound on the New York side, is an unforgettable experience. A majestic, graceful, powerful bridge, it is one of the preeminent engineering landmarks in the United States. Darl Rastorfer calls the George Washington Bridge "the most significant long-span suspension bridge of the twentieth century."

Built between 1927 and 1931, the "GW" connects Fort Lee, New Jersey, and New York City across the Hudson River. Unlike the suspension bridges crossing the Delaware River between New Jersey and Pennsylvania, this bridge has two decks to carry traffic. (Although part of the original design, the lower traffic deck, planned for light rail, was not added until 1962. Rastorfer notes that the bridge was designed "with a built-in capacity for expansion.") It also has higher towers (604 feet) and higher clearance at mid-span above mean high water (213 feet). Like the smaller Riegelsville Bridge, but unlike the Walt Whitman and Benjamin Franklin bridges, it has four cables, supplied by John A. Roebling's Sons Company. Each cable is 36 inches in diameter, made up of 61 strands of 26,474 individual wires, each wire having a diameter of .0196 inch. At the time it was built, the main span, at 3,500 feet, was twice the length of any existing suspension bridge span. The total length, anchorage to anchorage, is 4,760 feet. The concrete anchorage on the New York side weighs 260,010 tons; the anchorage on the New Jersey side is the trap rock of the Palisades. (The engineer, Othmar Ammann, and his architect, Cass Gilbert, had originally designed statuesque anchors, which were abandoned for cost reasons.) The George Washington Bridge was completed eight months ahead of schedule at a cost of $59 million. It remains one of the fifteen longest suspension bridges in the world (measured by center span), and is the oldest of the group.

The story behind the bridge has its share of intrigue and politics. On a certain level, it is the story of a mentor and a protégé, Gustav Lindenthal and Othmar Ammann. (Their relationship is discussed in some detail in the introduction.) Lindenthal was considered one of the preeminent engineers in the world during his career, which spanned approximately 1870 through 1933. His bridges included the Hell Gate (1916), the Blackwell's Island (Queensboro; 1909), the Manhattan (1909), and the Smithfield Street Bridge (1883) in Pittsburgh. He had been proposing designs for a suspension bridge over the Hudson River since perhaps 1887—more than thirty years before Ammann's plans were accepted. Following World War I, Lindenthal continued to press for a bridge crossing from midtown Manhattan to New Jersey; its cost of about $100 million was very reasonable, he argued, given that it would accommodate more vehicular and railroad traffic than the Holland Tunnel then under construction. However, various business interests in Manhattan, understandably unenthusiastic about having their property condemned or otherwise disrupted by bridge approaches, opposed the location.

Ammann was then Lindenthal's chief assistant. When in 1923 he proposed a less ambitious bridge farther north, at Fort Lee, Lindenthal roundly rebuked him. Ammann, then forty-four, opened his own engineering firm and proceeded to develop and refine his plan, which was presented in 1924 to the Connecticut Society of Engineers. It proposed eight lanes of traffic and two pedestrian walkways on

GEORGE WASHINGTON BRIDGE In this view, looking west toward New Jersey, the stunning towers of one of the most famous bridges in the world glint in the sunlight.

an upper deck, and four light-rail lines on a lower deck, all at a proposed cost of $40 million. Politically, Ammann's plan fit with the public works projects advocated by New Jersey Governor George Silzer, although it caused difficulties personally for Silzer, who was a business partner with Lindenthal in a New Jersey clay mine. Once Silzer threw his support to the Ammann proposal, business and other political interests fell into line. The legislatures of New York and New Jersey approved it in March 1925, and entrusted its construction to the Port Authority.

It is worth comparing the design approaches of Ammann and Lindenthal to lend perspective on why the former's design was deemed acceptable. Darl Rastorfer describes Lindenthal's design in terms of mass and heaviness; it relied on "deep chain trusses strung between its towers to prevent excessive motion on the road deck." By contrast, Ammann's design achieved that stability "through the design of the road deck itself." Ammann also built upon the mathematics and science of the "deflection theory," which was employed to some extent by Ralph Modjeski in engineering the Benjamin Franklin Bridge, as discussed earlier. Rastorfer believes that "Ammann was genuinely gambling when he applied deflection theory in the design" of this bridge, but he was justified by the economics. These calculations encouraged lighter bridges, saving on the cost of materials, and had an effect on the aesthetics as well, as reflected ultimately in the appearance of the George Washington Bridge towers.

However, Ammann had served on the commission investigating the failure of the first Quebec cantilever bridge, and he developed his own design for a pair of deep girders to stabilize the double deck. As Rastorfer puts it, Ammann derived "a corollary to the deflection theory that provided a statistical method of predicting aerodynamic stability" based on "the ratio of center span to side span to width and the effect of weight, cable sag, and stiffening girders." David Billington concurs: "What Ammann found when he looked at the results of the deflection theory and studied it carefully, was that the amount of force that would be in the horizontal truss was dependent not upon the loads, as one would normally think, but upon its stiffness. That means that if you reduce the stiffness, you reduce the forces in the truss. On that basis, Ammann realized that by making a much more slender truss for his two-deck bridge, he could save a very large amount of money." As Billington also observes, Ammann's reduction of materials was fully dependent upon constructing a safe bridge, with other factors of economics and aesthetics also relevant.

Ammann intended for the bridge to have granite towers, along the lines of the Brooklyn Bridge; aesthetically, they would appear as extensions of the natural stone of the Palisades on the New Jersey side and the granite outcroppings on the New York side. Noted architect Cass Gilbert (1858–1934) was enlisted to help design some stone ornamentation. When the Port Authority objected to the cost, Ammann's compromise was to use steel and cement, with steel providing the skeleton upon which the concrete would be added. That proposal was also abandoned because of cost and because Leon Moisseiff had redesigned the steel towers with sufficient strength to maintain the loads without the aid of concrete.

Another choice was between spun-wire cables, where wires are spun in the air from anchorage to anchorage, and eyebars, which are chains composed of thin metal bars bolted together at eyelets on each end. John A. Roebling's Sons Company was the winner of the competitive bid process, and its wire cables were used.

What had been known throughout its long journey to completion as the 179th Street Bridge or Hudson River Bridge was dedicated as the George Washington Bridge on October 25, 1931, in honor of the location's association with Washington and the upcoming bicentennial of his birth. Other names considered were Gate of Paradise, Bridge of Prosperity, Noble Experiment, Pride of the Nation, Peoples' Bridge, and Bi-State Bridge. New York Governor Franklin D. Roosevelt and New Jersey Governor Morgan F. Larson formally opened the bridge, and Lindenthal and Ammann arrived at the ceremonies together.

In *The Bridge*, the story of the Verrazano-Narrows Bridge, Gay Talese quotes Lilly Ammann on her husband's feelings about the George Washington: "That bridge is his firstborn, and it was a difficult birth. He'll always love it best." He then quotes Ammann himself: "It is as if you have a beautiful daughter and you are her father."

A Fort Lee Web site featuring the George Washington Bridge notes that an aviation beacon named for comedian Will Rogers and aviator Wiley Post was installed atop the tower on the New York side in 1935, and that the "Little Red Lighthouse" on the New York side in the shadow of the bridge became obsolete once navigational lights were placed on the bridge.

A glint of the personal politics surrounding this bridge could be seen as late as 1941. In that year David Steinman, Ammann's bitter rival, wrote that the George Washington Bridge is "the symbol of its civilization" and of the "young generation of Americans." Yet he refused to give full credit to Ammann, stating that the bridge was "designed and built by the Port of New York Authority under the direction of O. H. Ammann, with Cass Gilbert as consulting architect." Today, Ammann's achievement is fully recognized.

LUMBERVILLE PEDESTRIAN BRIDGE

The first bridge to cross the Delaware River from Raven Rock in New Jersey to Lumberville, Pennsylvania, was a covered one built between 1853 and 1856 by Solon Chapin, who, with James Madison Porter I, was responsible for the first bridge at Riegelsville to the north. Although approved by the legislatures of Pennsylvania and New Jersey in 1835–1836, construction on the Lumberville bridge did not begin until 1853, thus sparing it the disaster of the 1841 floods. This first bridge, built by the Lumberville Delaware River Bridge Company, had four spans and measured approximately 705 feet. Notwithstanding its luck in 1841, it was destroyed by later floods. The truss bridge that replaced it in 1903 was ultimately deemed unsafe. The current steel suspension bridge, 688 feet long and built in 1947

LUMBERVILLE
PEDESTRIAN BRIDGE   This suspension bridge is one of only two exclusively
pedestrian bridges across the Delaware River.
The other, the Portland-Columbia Bridge, is featured
in color plate 5.

by John A. Roebling's Sons Company, was designed solely for pedestrians on the determination that there was no need for a vehicular crossing here. Nearby is the Bull's Island Recreation Area and the Delaware and Raritan Canal.

DELAWARE MEMORIAL BRIDGE

Technically, two bridges operated by the Delaware River and Bay Authority cross the Delaware River: the first, built between 1949 and 1951 (now the eastbound route, carrying traffic from Delaware to New Jersey), and a parallel one, constructed from 1964 to 1968 (now the westbound route, from New Jersey to Delaware). They are 3,650 feet long and are separated by 250 feet. Each is a three-span bridge with a truss deck, and each carries four lanes of highway traffic. The engineer-designer was Othmar Ammann, who also designed the Bronx-Whitestone Bridge (1939) in New York and the George Washington Bridge. The original span was honored as the most beautiful large steel bridge of 1951 by the American Institute of Steel Construction.

The successful opening of the Benjamin Franklin Bridge in 1926 proved the feasibility of suspension crossings over the Delaware River. In that same year a ferry was established at the future site of the Delaware Memorial Bridge between Pennsville, New Jersey, and New Castle, Delaware, as a temporary solution until a bridge could be built. A study was authorized by the Delaware General Assembly in 1940, but the outbreak of World War II delayed further action until 1947, when construction was approved. Like other large bridges proposed across significant rivers, this one faced opposition from those who saw a threat to shipping interests, in this case, Philadelphia port authorities. Another major opponent was the Department of War, which argued that the bridge would be a vulnerable target and block access to the Navy yard at Philadelphia. These objections lost out to increasingly urgent traffic demands. The two state legislatures authorized a bridge, and Congress passed enabling legislation in 1946. Among the contractors was the ubiquitous American Bridge Company, whose involvement included work on the New Jersey approach, construction of the footbridge, and hoisting of the main span bottom chord to fit on the south truss.

The total length of the bridges, including the approaches, is 13,200 feet. The towers, which rise 417 feet above mean high water, are sleek, simple, and elegant.

Ammann repeated their portal shape in his design of the Verrazano-Narrows Bridge (1964). The 188-foot clearance above mean high water at center satisfied military requirements for allowing tall ships to pass. The foundations of the towers are caissons, each of which contains about 27,000 tons of concrete. The four anchorages used 23,200 tons of concrete each. Both bridges have two twenty-inch-diameter cables, with 8,284 wires per cable.

Although some people favored building a second bridge farther south, the increased cost of new road construction argued in favor of a "twin" set of bridges. The original bridge cost $44 million to build; more than ten years later, the second bridge cost $77 million. When completed in 1951, the first bridge was the sixth-longest suspension bridge in the world. Today, more than twenty-five suspension bridges are longer.

The Delaware Memorial Bridge is a significant link between the New Jersey Turnpike and Interstate 295 to the east and north, and to Interstate 95 and the southern express route. Interestingly, in 2001—the fiftieth anniversary of the first span—the bridge's toll superintendent, Raymond DiCamillo, referred to the bridge as a part of a roadway connection between Washington, D.C., and the United Nations in New York. The bridges are dedicated to American war veterans, and there is a war memorial area near the bridge, including a reflective pool and statue.

DELAWARE MEMORIAL BRIDGE   The view from Carney's Point showcases the elegance of Othmar Ammann's design.

As noted elsewhere in this book, people sometimes die during the construction of a bridge. According to Steve Anderson, four men lost their lives building the first Delaware Memorial Bridge, and several others were reportedly killed on the second when a concrete form ruptured. In *The Bridge*, his account of the Verrazano-Narrows Bridge, Gay Talese focuses on the men who actually drive the rivets and spin the cables, the men who work from high above the river and build the bridge. He also interviewed the bridge's designer. Ammann told him that "one reason he has experienced no tragedy with his bridges is that he has been blessed with good fortune":

> "I have been lucky," he said, quietly.
>
> "Lucky!" snapped his wife, who attributes his success solely to his superior mind.
>
> "Lucky," he repeated, silencing her with his soft, hard tone of authority.

Engineering history is filled with the stories of successful engineers building many acclaimed bridges, only to have their reputations destroyed by the one that fails, despite all their caution. Ammann served on the commission that investigated the collapse of the first Quebec Bridge in 1907, and apparently learned well the dangers of underestimating the need to protect a bridge from stress. On the Delaware Memorial Bridge—as on his Walt Whitman Bridge, Throgs Neck Bridge, and Verrazano-Narrows Bridge—he employed deep stiffening trusses to ensure against the vertical force of load and the horizontal force of wind.

WALT WHITMAN BRIDGE

In the last years of his life, American poet Walt Whitman (1819–1892) lived at 330 Mickle Street in Camden, in a house that still stands. Of the ferry that in those days took people from Camden to Philadelphia, he wrote in *Specimen Days*, in a chapter titled "Scenes on Ferry and River—Last Winter's Nights": "What exhilaration, change, people, business, by day. What soothing, silent, wondrous hours, at night, crossing on the boat, 'most all to myself—pacing the deck, alone, forward or aft. What communion with the waters, the air, the exquisite *chiaroscuro*—the sky and stars, that speak no word, nothing to the intellect, yet so eloquent, so communicative to the soul."

WALT WHITMAN BRIDGE   Perhaps in keeping with its "common man" namesake, the Walt Whitman connects to an industrial area south of Camden.

This personal appreciation of the ferry contrasts with the public controversy that surrounded construction of the bridge that bears Whitman's name. The bridge proposal put forward in 1950 by the Philadelphia City Planning Commission met with little of the enthusiasm that greeted the Benjamin Franklin Bridge. On the New Jersey side, both Gloucester City and Camden opposed it, contending that a four-lane tunnel would require less costly right-of-way acquisitions and not have so negative an impact environmentally on the surrounding area. Pushing forward, however, the newly established Delaware River Port Authority secured the permission of the Army Corps of Engineers in 1952, and construction began shortly afterward. The bridge eventually cost $90 million to build.

The other source of controversy was the bridge's name. The same special committee that renamed the Delaware River Bridge for Benjamin Franklin chose to honor Camden's famous citizen-poet and author of *Leaves of Grass*. (Ironically, the bridge is actually located in Gloucester City.) The Catholic Diocese of Camden and other New Jersey politicians opposed the decision because they believed Whitman to have been homosexual. The Camden County Freeholders even floated the very plain "Gloucester Bridge" as an alternative. In the end, the opposition was not sufficient to overcome the support for the name. The dedication occurred on May 15, 1957, with governors and local politicians in attendance.

Othmar Ammann was a design consultant for the Walt Whitman Bridge and was also responsible for the Delaware Memorial Bridge, the Verrazano-Narrows Bridge, and the Throgs Neck Bridge. Like those bridges, as Steve Anderson observes, the Walt Whitman has "deep stiffening trusses and streamlined towers." Also involved in the design was Frank Masters, of Modjeski and Masters; William Shank gives design credit to this firm without mentioning Ammann. Ralph Modjeski was no stranger to the Delaware River, having designed the Benjamin Franklin and Tacony-Palmyra bridges. The architectural firm involved with the bridge, Harbeson, Hough, Livingston, and Larson, was established by former students and associates of Paul P. Cret, who had been the architect on the Ben Franklin Bridge. Darl Rastorfer notes that many of the union bridge builders ("boomers") who worked on the Walt Whitman were later involved with construction of the Verrazano-Narrows Bridge.

Although, at 2,000 feet, the Walt Whitman is somewhat longer, tower to tower, than the Ben Franklin (1,750 feet), its two cables are smaller (a diameter of twenty-three inches versus thirty). The towers are 378 feet above mean water and use caisson foundations. Consistent with War Department considerations, the clearance at center over mean water is 150 feet.

Now perhaps overshadowed by Camden to the north, Gloucester City was the site of the first European settlement on the east bank of the Delaware River. The Dutch explorer Cornelius Jacobsen Mey built Fort Nassau here in 1623, although a permanent settlement was not fully established until the arrival of Irish Quakers in 1682.

MOVABLE BRIDGES

Movable bridges, as the name implies, change position in whole or in part to allow traffic to pass below or around them. The concept is not new. As early as the sixteenth century, Leonardo da Vinci designed a "very light yet rugged" movable bridge for military purposes. The basic types are the bascule, swing, and lift bridges.

A familiar kind of bascule bridge is the drawbridge, in which a single leaf or each of two opposing leaves has a counterbalance at one end (bascule means "balance" or "see-saw" in French). When the counterbalance is allowed to sink, the free end rises on a horizontal axis. A double-leaf bascule has two ends that rise and form an inverted "V" to allow marine traffic to pass. A variation of the bascule bridge is the rolling lift; as the the leaf rises into the upright position, it rolls on a bearing instead of rotating on an axis.

The swing bridge rotates ninety degrees on a vertical axis on a central pivot pier, allowing marine traffic to pass on either side. Swing bridges are usually employed for railroad crossings. The movable span is supported either by a center bearing on a vertical pin or pivot, or by a rim bearing on a "drum" that is a circular girder. The latter configuration was generally used for wider and heavier bridges. Swing bridges were moved, depending upon size and date of fabrication, by hand crank, steam engine, or electric motors, with gears and rack-and-pinion drives. Although the swing bridge is often considered in a category of its own, the structure itself can employ truss or girder construction. Lichtenstein Consulting Engineers of Paramus, New Jersey, a firm that has reported on historic bridges for the Delaware Department of Transportation and for the New Jersey Historic Bridge Survey, observes that swing bridges date back to at least the seventeenth century in Europe. The firm notes that "[t]he demise of swing span bridges . . . resulted from the basic problem that the movable span and pivot pier are obstructions to navigation." One such bridge in New Jersey that is scheduled for replacement by a high-clearance bridge is the Victory Bridge over the Raritan River near Perth Amboy and Sayreville (color plate 16).

The lift bridge, as its name implies, operates like an elevator, with the entire span rising vertically between towers. In *Landmarks on the Iron Road*, William Middleton observes that they were preferred for railroad traffic, "particularly where long clear spans were required." He explains how they work: "The weight of the lift span was counterbalanced by weights attached to each end through cables running over sheaves at the top of each tower. Lift spans reached some prodigious dimensions."

One now obsolete type of movable bridge was the "retractile" bridge from the mid-nineteenth century. The 1997 Contextual Study of New York State's Pre-1961 Bridges describes it as a bridge where the span moves horizontally onto the roadway. Although efficient, it required a fair amount of land to operate, and did not survive as a popular form. A twentieth-century development was the pontoon bridge, a movable bridge that serves as a temporary crossing.

The original movable bridges were the drawbridges of medieval times, raised by ropes and pulleys. The earliest timber swing bridges rotated around a pier to provide channels for passage of vessels on either side. Steel and metal replaced timber in swing bridges beginning in the nineteenth century, and eventually motorized mechanisms were used in place of manual cranking mechanisms. The bascule bridge became more popular than the swing bridge at the onset of the twentieth century, taking advantage of the efficiencies of metal girders and concrete counterweights. They could be constructed in narrower waterways and more congested urban settings than the swing bridges.

The modern era of the bascule bridge is deemed to begin in 1893 with the Van Buren Street Bridge in Chicago, a rolling lift bridge built on the design patented by William Scherzer. In this type of bridge, the center of rotation shifts as the rotating part moves horizontally on a track. The Shark River Bridge in Belmar, New Jersey (discussed below with the Oceanic Bridge), was built by Scherzer's company but is not a rolling lift bridge. Rather, it is a simple trunnion bascule, a design that the Lichtenstein firm describes as not typical of the company's work. The trunnion bascule has a fixed point of rotation and center of gravity, near the end of the leaf, with the counterweight at the end. The easiest way understand this design is to imagine a seesaw with the trunnion (a horizontal steel pivot) as the fulcrum of the seesaw, but placed nearly at the end, with a heavy weight on the short end of the seesaw to create enough weight to raise the longer end.

Regardless of efficiencies in operation and cost, bascule bridges nevertheless cause delays in traffic. Yet the higher-span bridges preferred by today's road engineers can be expensive to build, due to the need for the approaches, and they may not always be feasible within the physical constraints of a particular site.

Gerald Oliveto's railroad-related Web site identifies thirty-three movable railroad bridges in New Jersey (a thirty-fourth, in the Camden area, has been noted by another reader). Of those cited by Oliveto, seventeen are swing, six vertical lift, nine bascule (angular), and one an "A" frame. He includes the Delair and Arthur Kill lift bridges discussed below, but also counts some that are no longer in use or that are kept in a permanently open position. One of these, an abandoned bascule railroad bridge in Newark, is featured in color plate 2.

DELAIR LIFT BRIDGE

This 500-foot lift bridge (horizontal clearance), with a main span of 165 feet and camelback trusses, was built in 1895–1896 by the Pennsylvania Railroad Company across the Delaware River at Delair, New Jersey, to accommodate Pennsylvanians traveling to resorts on the Jersey shore, including Atlantic City. It was the first bridge constructed over the Delaware River south of Trenton, and it has a vertical clearance of 135 feet (49 feet when the bridge is lowered). Total length is about 4,400 feet. The HAER notes that it is a "riveted Warren truss vertical-lift span; pin-connected Petit through truss; riveted trestle bent; riveted deck girder."

William Middleton writes that in 1960 the American Bridge Company floated a replacement truss into position for this bridge. This floating method was preferable to the more expensive falsework needed to sustain the truss in position until it was ready to stay supported.

DELAIR LIFT BRIDGE   This railroad lift bridge is shown in its down position.

The bridge is unique, according to HAER, for "the world's heaviest center-bearing swing span" and "longest double-track vertical-lift span," both still present. At the time of its construction, it attracted global attention.

NEWARK SWING BRIDGES

The Passaic River begins at about 600 feet above sea level around Mendham, New Jersey, and runs ninety miles to empty into Newark Bay. It drops 77 feet at the Great Falls in Paterson, and it is navigable by oceangoing vessels to the rapids above Passaic.

In 1795 two toll bridges were built in Newark across the Passaic and Hackensack rivers. The Passaic one was 492 feet long, and the Hackensack one, 980 feet. According to Norman Brydon, the builder was Josiah Nottage, who also constructed the Charles River Bridge between Boston and Cambridge. The Newark bridges were so popular that citizens protested the toll charges as excessive. (Few things in political life are really new.) A plaque at the junction of Broad and Bridge streets in Newark proclaims, "[T]he bridging of the rivers eastward and the rude road built across the marsh was an enterprise of patriotic citizens; an epoch-making event. It awoke the industries and made the present city possible." In his history of Newark, John T. Cunningham cites an early source that describes the road connecting these two bridges; it was made of multiple layers of logs "covered with sod and earth dug up on each side" and overlaid with gravel.

Today, three steel swing bridges for vehicular traffic operate on the Passaic River in Newark within relatively close proximity of one another. They are (with their dates of construction) the Jackson Street (1897–1898), Clay Street (1908), and Bridge Street (1913) bridges. They were built largely during the period of Newark's history when the city was led by Mayor Julius A. Lebkuecher, who, according to Cunningham, aimed to combine the goals of economy and efficiency with beautification. These bridges should be seen as part of the same response to the industrialization of Newark that led to the paving of roads and other efforts to improve transportation.

The Jackson Street and Clay Street bridges were designed by James Owens, the county engineer, but records do not identify the designer of the Bridge Street Bridge. The New Jersey Historic Bridge Survey, largely citing county records, provides much of the information presented here. The HAER features the Jackson Street Bridge.

CLAY STREET BRIDGE   This is one of the three swing bridges that carry vehicular traffic over the Passaic River in Newark.

A local contractor, A. E. Sandford Company, built the 326-foot Clay Street Bridge, which is a three-span Warren through truss. The Jackson Street Bridge was constructed by the McCann Fagan Iron Works. This curved chord lattice through-truss bridge is 710 feet in length. Both of these swing bridges were originally powered by steam engines.

The 371-foot Bridge Street Bridge, built by the American Bridge Company, has a Pratt through truss and is supported on an ashlar substructure with concrete caps. The swing span turns on wheels attached to the bottom of a drum girder inside the track. Automation of the bridge's manual rotation system in 1981 raised a safety concern. Because the process could not be stopped once it started, the new system was dismantled. The swing span and substructure are considered historically significant because they represent one of the few such systems that continues to operate.

Between the Bridge Street Bridge and the William J. Stickel Memorial Bridge to its north, the Newark Drawbridge accommodates rail traffic (see color plate 9). A center-bearing swing bridge over the Passaic River, the Newark Drawbridge was built in 1903 by the Delaware, Lackawanna, and Western Railroad. (New Jersey Transit refers to its movable bridges generically as drawbridges.) According to New Jersey Transit's Historic Railroad Bridge Survey, this bridge is significant because its "innovative methods" of construction and installation "received national attention." It is also "an unusual example of a two-level swing bridge, designed with two main through tracks on the upper level and a single freight track below."

FEDERAL STREET BRIDGE

According to a Web site devoted to the streets of Camden, Federal Street was originally called Joseph Cooper's Lane. Joshua Cooper, a member of the prominent family that operated Cooper's Ferry, renamed the lane in 1803 in honor of the Federalist Party. Federal Street became a major east-west route, ending at the Delaware River and the ferry landing. The original ferry at the site was operated by William Roydon. According to Jeffrey Dorwart, William Cooper bought out Roydon's license in 1688, and the Cooper family thereafter enjoyed a monopoly on ferry service between Camden Town and Philadelphia.

The Federal Street Bridge was built in 1906 by the Strauss Bascule Bridge Company, which invented this type of span and built its first one in Cleveland, Ohio, in 1905. Although the single-leaf Federal Street Bridge is only 134 feet in length, it has been described by the New Jersey Historic Bridge Survey "as one of the most architectonic bridge[s] in the state." Moreover, the survey deems it "one of the most significant moveable span bridges in the state because of its date of

FEDERAL STREET
BRIDGE

This outstanding example of Beaux-Arts construction is described by the Historic Bridge Survey as "an expression of the City Beautiful philosophy of civic projects."
The metal movable span portion seen at the bottom left is a 78-foot rivet-connected Warren pony truss.
The overhead counterweight, used to lever the bridge upward, is supported by steel columns and includes the operator's house beneath a double-level concrete veneer.

construction, type, embellishments, and state of preservation." In 1999 the New Jersey Department of Environmental Protection, Historic Preservation Office, authorized the bridge's rehabilitation so that it would "continue to reflect an age when the City of Camden's contributions to arts and industry were paramount in South Jersey." When completed in 2003, the work received the New Jersey Historic Preservation Award, among other distinctions. The Federal Street Bridge is indeed a striking monument in the middle of an otherwise depressed-looking industrial area.

The overhead concrete counterweight is a good example of the Beaux-Arts style of architectural design and decoration popular during the "City Beautiful" movement of the late nineteenth and early twentieth centuries. That political, cultural, and architectural movement originated in the "White City" designed for the Chicago Columbian Exposition of 1893 and presented an alternative to the squalidness of city life made public and vivid by such artists and literary activists as Jacob Riis, Theodore Dreiser, and Stephen Crane. "Beaux Arts" ("fine arts" in French) refers to the philosophy of the Ecole des Beaux-Arts in Paris, a school of architecture that advanced a style that made use of classical concepts of grandeur to create monumental, orderly buildings. Today, the Federal Street Bridge stands out in its surroundings as an inspiration to continued efforts to regain the promise of a better future that its opening must have represented a century ago.

COURT STREET BRIDGE

This 317-foot-long Warren truss steel center-bearing swing bridge, with riveted connections, crosses the Hackensack River between Hackensack and Bogota. It was built in 1907–1908 by F. R. Long and Company, which did so much business in Bergen County that it relocated its corporate headquarters there in 1899. The bridge was designed by R. Earle, the county engineer, a fact that again highlights the contributions of local professionals to the overall transportation needs of the state.

Hackensack was officially incorporated in 1868, but the community's history reaches back to 1647, when the Dutch from Manhattan established a trading post known as New Barbadoes. A few minutes' walk from the Court Street Bridge is

COURT STREET BRIDGE   The distinctive dome of the Bergen County
Courthouse rises in the background of this view.

The Green, where both American and British soldiers camped during the Revolution. Lida Newberry notes that the Church on the Green (First Dutch Reformed), built in 1696 and rebuilt in 1728, is one of the oldest in the state. Also nearby are the imposing courthouse (1912) and the U.S.S. *Ling*, a World War II submarine moored at the New Jersey Naval Museum. Hackensack derives its name from the Achkincheshacky Indians, whose chief, Oratam, welcomed the original Dutch settlers.

The New Jersey Historic Bridge Survey describes the Court Street Bridge as a "well-preserved example" of "one of several swing-span crossings of the Hackensack River, an important navigable waterway instrumental in the growth and industrial development of Bergen County." It replaced an earlier swing bridge at the same site.

At the opposite end of the state, in Camden, the State Street Bridge over the Cooper River (color plate 14) is another example of a Warren truss swing span. Built in 1898, it is, according to the Historic Bridge Survey, "one of the most complete nineteenth-century highway thru truss centerbearing swing spans in the state."

WITTPENN BRIDGE

The steel lift bridge that carries Route 7 across the Hackensack River between Jersey City and Kearny was constructed between 1927 and 1930 at a cost of $3 million. When lowered, the main span rests 35 feet above mean high water, ascending to 100 feet above water when raised. The main lift span is only 83 feet in length; but when its viaduct approaches are considered, the bridge has a total length of 2,169 feet. The piers and decks are made of reinforced concrete.

On or near this site on the Hackensack River, a bridge replaced Douw's Ferry in 1795. Much later, a swing bridge built here in 1909 made way for the Wittpenn. Sigvald Johannesson, designer of the Pulaski Skyway, served as design engineer for the Wittpenn, with consulting services from the engineering firm of Harrington Howard and Ash.

The bridge takes its name from the New Jersey state highway commissioner who cut the ribbon to open it in 1930. H. Otto Wittpenn was a one-time political rival of President Woodrow Wilson, who appointed him comptroller of customs in New York. As mayor of Jersey City from 1908 to 1913, Wittpenn had been an ally of political boss Frank Hague, but Hague opposed Wittpenn's bid for the governorship in 1916. Hague's failure to support his fellow Democrat helped the Republican Party win the election. Interestingly, Hague, who won the mayorship of Jersey City in 1917, later supported George Silzer, the New Jersey governor who became Othmar Ammann's patron in gaining approval of his design for the George Washington Bridge project.

The Hackensack River begins in Rockland County, New York, and empties into Newark Bay. It is approximately forty-five miles long and navigable by oceangoing vessels as far as Kearny, and then by tugboat and barge to Hackensack. Sadly, it was listed as a Most Endangered River in 1996.

Also endangered is the Wittpenn Bridge. Steve Anderson reports that it is nearing the end of its life and that plans are in the making to replace it with a drawbridge (confirmed on the NJDOT Web site). It is thus part of the historical record captured in this book. Currently, the bridge is part of the Hackensack River Lift Bridges Historic District, which includes the Lower Hackensack Bridge, the Wittpenn Bridge, the Pennsylvania Harsimus Branch Bridge, and the Pennsylvania Railroad (now PATH) Bridge between Kearny and Jersey City.

Two more bridges whose obituaries will soon be written are the William J. Stickel Memorial Bridge across the Passaic River in Newark (color plate 9) and the

WITTPENN BRIDGE   Almost Gothic in appearance when silhouetted against
the sky, this lift bridge is reminiscent of a cathedral.

Victory Bridge over the Raritan near Perth Amboy and Sayreville (color plate 16). The Stickel Bridge, which carries Interstate 280, was named after a one-time Essex County engineer, making it one of the few bridges to bear such a tribute. (The Morris Goodkind Bridge, discussed previously, is another.) Although it is relatively young, having been built in 1949, the Stickel Bridge was labeled obsolete and structurally deficient in an April 2001 study by the New Jersey Department of Transportation. At the time of this writing, the Victory Bridge was being replaced by a new, high-clearance girder bridge and the renovated Edison Bridge (color plate 15).

These bridges, like the railroad bridges mentioned in the discussion of the Newark swing bridges, establish distinctive silhouettes against the sky. Their overwhelming, dark, and massive presence reminds us of the industrial supremacy that the United States has commanded. Space does not permit images or discussion of all of them, and others may be seen along the rivers and highways of the state.

DORSET AVENUE BRIDGE

Built in 1929–1930, the Dorset Avenue Bridge is a 220-foot steel double-leaf trunnion bascule across the Inside Thorofare boat channel from Ventnor City to Ventnor Heights in Atlantic County. (Its main span is bascule; its approaches are girders.) The four two-story towers house the operator and storage, and include a machinery room and rest room. The Inside Thorofare channel divides Chelsea Heights and Ventnor Heights on the west and Absecon Island on the east, where the resort towns of Atlantic City, Ventnor, Margate, and Longport attract visitors.

A plaque on the bridge refers to it as a "Strauss Bascule" and names Alexander H. Nelson as engineer. J. B. Strauss (1870–1938) received a patent in 1911 for the "articulated counterweight bridge" that proved successful for his company. According to the New Jersey Historic Bridge Survey, the Dorset Avenue Bridge is an example of "an increasingly rare movable bridge technology patented by the Strauss Bascule Bridge Company." The only other example of a double-leaf bascule in Atlantic County is in Margate City, where Mill Road (County Road 563) crosses Beach Thorofare to Absecon Island. Elsewhere in New Jersey, Strauss also designed, and F. W. Schuierl built, the 307-foot, three-span, double-leaf Market Street Bridge across the Passaic River in Passaic. Owing to major modifications, that bridge is not deemed historically significant.

DORSET AVENUE BRIDGE   Part of Atlantic City's skyline is visible in the background.

A single-leaf bascule bridge built in 1924 carries Route 9 over the Bass River in Bass River Township, Burlington County, and another one in Mullica Township takes the Egg Harbor–Green Bank Road over the Mullica River. Both of these bridges were constructed by the J. B. Strauss Company. A contemporary of these bridges in the northern part of the state, the single-leaf Eighth Street Bridge over the Passaic River in Passaic City, was designed by the Strauss Bascule Bridge Company and built in 1915 by the F. R. Long–W. G. Broadhunt Company.

The Dorset Avenue Bridge is one of the terminus points for the annual Seacat Bridge-to-Bridge Bay Swim in August. The race, begun in 1999, consists of either a 1.3-mile swim from the bridge to the Albany Avenue Bridge in Atlantic City or a five-kilometer run from Albany Avenue to Dorset Avenue and back.

BURLINGTON-BRISTOL BRIDGE

Burlington, capital of the province of West Jersey, was a significant point on the colonial route from New York to Philadelphia. Queen Anne granted the original ferry charter at this site early in the eighteenth century, and almost two centuries would pass before a bridge was constructed here. A major concern was the need to allow marine traffic to reach factories as far north as Trenton. In the original proposals, a bridge would have crossed from Market Street in Bristol, Pennsylvania, to St. Mary Street in Burlington, New Jersey, via Burlington Island in the middle of the river. The plan finally approved by the War Department over the opposition of the ferry operator relocated the bridge south to Maple Beach in Bristol and Reed Street in Burlington.

The steel vertical-lift Burlington-Bristol Bridge was built in 1930–1931. The Burlington County Bridge Commission puts its length at 2,301 feet from abutment to abutment, with a 61-foot vertical clearance at high tide beneath the main lift span that crosses the Delaware River. The 540-foot main span was the longest of its kind at the time of its construction. It is raised by two 80-horsepower electric motors.

Steve Anderson's phillyroads.com Web site offers different statistics for the bridge. He assigns it a total length of 3,144 feet, including the approaches, allowing 940 feet for the main span (540 feet) and two side spans (200 feet each). He reports that the clearance to mean high water is 138 feet when the lift span is

BURLINGTON-BRISTOL BRIDGE   A view from the promenade in Burlington, looking westward across the Delaware to Pennsylvania.

raised, and 35 feet when lowered. Anderson also writes that "the vertical lift span was considered a modern design when it was built." The bridge has a look different from that of the Delair or Arthur Kill lift bridges, or even the Wittpenn, perhaps because its towers do not dominate the overall appearance of the bridge.

Like the Tacony-Palmyra Bridge discussed elsewhere, the Burlington-Bristol is a composite bridge. In addition to the lift element, it has through-truss spans, stringer spans, and deck truss spans. Both bridges are owned and managed by the Burlington County Bridge Commission, and both were the subject of extended legal proceedings, resulting in the return of the $3 million profit their private owners reaped from their questionable sale to a county agency.

The Burlington County Bridge Commission is also responsible for the Riverside-Delanco Bridge, a movable bridge over Rancocas Creek. This pony truss is the third bridge built on the site, following a bow truss bridge in 1870 and a Warren truss in 1901. Its vertical clearance over the water is a mere twelve feet. Among the minor bridges under the jurisdiction of the Burlington County Bridge Commission are the Pennsauken Creek Bridge, the Route 73 Overpass, Pompeston Creek Bridge, Swede Run Bridge, and Twin Pipe Culvert.

Burlington was founded in 1677 by two companies of Quakers, one from Yorkshire and one from London. High Street was originally laid out with lots to the east for the Yorkshiremen and lots to the west for Londoners. In addition to its important role in New Jersey's colonial history, Burlington was the birthplace of James Fenimore Cooper in 1789 and of James ("Don't Give Up the Ship") Lawrence in 1781. Their homes still stand and today operate as museums. The stately Boudinot House was built by Elias Boudinot, who was president of the Continental Congress and therefore, in a real way, of the fledgling United States. Also of note is the so-called General Grant House, where Grant sent his family to live during the Civil War and where, supposedly, he was in residence the night Abraham Lincoln was assassinated.

OCEANIC BRIDGE

This 2,712-foot, fifty-seven-span steel double-leaf bascule bridge across the Navesink River between Rumson and Middletown was built in 1939 as one of the many Depression-era public-works projects of the Works Progress Administration (WPA). In New Jersey, this New Deal federal agency hired unemployed workers to undertake many needed structures, including schools, courthouses, post offices,

OCEANIC BRIDGE   The distinctive towers of this bridge make it a landmark on the Navesink River.

and highways. The WPA paid 45 percent of the construction cost of the Oceanic Bridge.

A through-truss swing bridge, built in 1891, operated at this site until it deteriorated in the 1930s. The new bridge was designed by Ash Howard Needles and Tammen, a firm known for its movable bridges. The principal members of the firm had trained under J.A.L. Waddell, the engineer responsible for the Goethals Bridge and Outerbridge Crossing. New Jersey's state bridge engineer, Morris Goodkind, was a consultant. The Historic Bridge Survey calls this bridge "one of the most architectonic and technologically distinguished twentieth-century double leaf bascule bridges in New Jersey." Its two operator's houses have distinctive vertical bars at the windows.

Louis R. Ash, a member of the design firm, obtained a patent in 1927 for a center lock for bascule bridges. As described in that patent, the principal object of his device was "to lock the movable span or spans in traffic carrying position uniformly at various points in the width of the bridge, to effect the locking at the various points synchronously and to control the locking and unlocking operation from a point distant from the lock and its operating mechanism."

Another example of a bascule bridge is the Shark River Bridge, built in 1927 in Belmar by the Scherzer Rolling Lift Bridge Company. Essentially, it is a simple trunnion bascule bridge rather than the rolling lift type promised by the company's name. "Rolling lift" bridges were more commonly used for railroad bridges, and the Scherzer company did in fact construct several in New Jersey.

——————— ARTHUR KILL LIFT BRIDGE

With a length of 558 feet, the main (center) span of the Arthur Kill Lift Bridge remains the longest in the world by about 7 feet. According to Judith Dupré, it is followed by the al-Firdan Bridge over the Suez Canal in Egypt (1963) and the Cape Cod Canal Railroad Bridge in Massachusetts (544 feet, built 1933–1935). This single-track, vertical lift railroad bridge has two 215-foot-high towers. When raised, the lift portion ascends 135 feet above mean water level. The bridge was built by the Baltimore and Ohio Railroad (B&O) to connect Elizabeth, New Jersey, to Staten Island, and it opened in 1959.

Elizabeth is one of the underappreciated cities of New Jersey, at least from a historical perspective. The oldest English settlement in New Jersey (1664), it was the provincial capital and the site, in 1668, of the first general assembly. With a waterfront on Newark Bay, the city was a significant industrial center by the end of the seventeenth century, but the Revolution arrested its progress. Matters picked up in 1835, when a group of New York businessmen purchased land and began planning the port facilities here. By the end of the nineteenth century, major industries, such as the Singer Sewing Machine Company, had established a presence in Elizabeth.

In *The Bridges of New York*, Sharon Reier describes the background to the construction of the Arthur Kill Lift Bridge. Throughout the second half of the nineteenth century, Staten Islanders had sought alternative connections to the mainland because the Staten Island–New York ferry runs were insufficient, and a link to Bayonne was considered advantageous. Opposition from ferry owners and individuals who liked the isolation delayed the bridging of the island until the B&O acquired the Staten Island Rapid Transit system in 1885 and built the first railroad bridge over the Arthur Kill (an eight-hundred-foot swing bridge) in 1890. In 1959 the lift bridge replaced the older swing bridge.

ARTHUR KILL LIFT BRIDGE   Part of a comprehensive solution to the
transportation needs of this waterway,
the Arthur Kill Lift Bridge, shown here in its
raised position, is one of the largest movable
bridges in the world.

William Middleton notes that a lift bridge was chosen because of the increased
amount of marine traffic. The old swing bridge was an impediment to the twenty-
four hundred marine vessels passing there each month. Middleton describes the
Pratt truss of the replacement bridge:

> Each end of the lift span was supported by 40 wire ropes, each 2¼ inch in
> diameter, which passed across four 15-foot diameter cast steel sheaves at the
> top of each tower to counterweights that were made up of steel boxes filled
> with concrete. Each sheave weighed 23 tons and was carried on two roller
> bearings. An auxiliary counterweight system compensated for the unbalanced
> weight of the cablers as the counterweights moved up or down.

The American Bridge Company built the superstructure, which was fabricated at its Ambridge, Pennsylvania, factory, assembled on Staten Island, and
floated into position. One tower has an operator's house, and both have flashing
aerial beacons.

Like the Pulaski Skyway, the Arthur Kill Lift Bridge presents stark black lines against a numbingly industrial background, making it a beautiful counterpoint in the environment. Another example of the beauty of strong bridge lines is the scene across Newark Bay, viewed from Bayonne, which includes a railroad lift bridge (color plate 3).

GIRDER BRIDGES

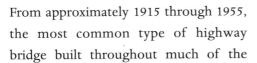

From approximately 1915 through 1955, the most common type of highway bridge built throughout much of the United States was the steel girder bridge. The girder is a form of beam bridge in which the deck slab is supported by certain types of beams or girders. Wooden timbers were shaped into girders until iron, steel, and reinforced concrete came along. Following World War II and the expansion of highway systems, steel-and-concrete girder bridges became commonplace. Donald Jackson notes their advantage in providing "solid, stable crossings capable of withstanding fast-moving traffic." On the other hand, a girder bridge is a material-intensive structure and therefore more costly than a truss bridge of comparable size.

Two basic types of girder bridges will be described: the I-beam and the box. Other, less common girder types take the shape of the Greek letter *Pi* (Π) or the capital T. On occasion, a girder bridge may be curved in an effort to resemble an arch. The I-beam consists of two flanges (top and bottom plates) welded to the web (side plate), so that when viewed from the end, head-on, it resembles the capital letter I. It is also called the plate girder. Most highway bridges are the "slab-on-stringer" type, basically, a concrete-and-steel beam bridge.

The box girder is just that—a box formed by four plates welded into a box shape, with the flanges on the top and bottom, and the webs forming the sides.

When more than two webs are used, the girder is said to be multi-chambered. Because of their stability, box girders are used for spanning longer distances than I-beam girders. They are supported in the same manner as a beam or continuous-beam bridge. The first box girder bridges were designed by Robert Stephenson in north Wales: the Conway Tubular Bridge (1848) and the Britannia Tubular Bridge (1850). Demetrios Tonias, in *Bridge Engineering*, writes that "[w]hen bending and torsion are major concerns, a box girder type structure offers an aesthetically pleasing, albeit expensive, solution." The extra expense arises because such bridges are not standardized or prefabricated.

An analysis prepared by Ashok Gupta and Sachin Dhir of the Department of Civil Engineering, Indian Institute of Technology, Delhi, compared the advantages and disadvantages of girder forms. I-beam girder bridges generally have a straightforward mathematical analysis, lower fabrication costs, ease of construction, and lighter sections than box girders. But larger exposed areas leave them more susceptible to the elements than box girders. Also, they have less aesthetic appeal because of bracing requirements, and they make less efficient use of web material. The T-beam shares the geometric simplicity of the I-beam, can generally be fabricated with local materials at the construction site, facilitates slab interaction, and has fewer longitudinal members than I-beams. On the other hand, like the I-beam, the T-beam is not the most aesthetic structure and is heavier than even the I-beam. Nevertheless, box girders, Gupta and Dhir note, "have been widely used as economic and aesthetic solutions for overcrossing, undercrossing, separation structures and viaducts found in today's modern highway systems." Made of "single or multi-cell reinforced and prestressed concrete," box girders have numerous advantages: torsional strength, ability to accommodate curved bridges, less need for construction depth (as opposed to I-beams and T-beams), fewer maintenance issues, and more aesthetic appeal. On the negative side, they are heavy and inefficient for smaller spans.

Some critics might be tempted to dismiss the possibility of any aesthetic value in the ever-present girder bridge. But we should look past their seeming commonality and consider them in broader terms, as Elizabeth Mock has done. She observes that the girder bridge "is a good, simple elementary form, orderly and restful, and at its best—shallow, cleanly drawn, crisply detailed—it is not only pleasantly unobtrusive but notably elegant." In particular, two examples of girder bridges in New Jersey were significant when they were first constructed, and we should not take their achievements for granted.

The Portland-Columbia Pedestrian Bridge (color plate 5) is one of only two pedestrian bridges spanning the Delaware River. Built in 1957–1958, it replaced a covered bridge that in its own day was one of the most advanced bridges built across that river. The current 770-foot, four-span steel girder bridge provides scenic views of the Delaware River Viaduct to the north.

According to the New Jersey Historic Bridge Survey, the Edison Bridge (color plate 15), built between 1938 and 1940 across the Raritan River, is "an early example of a large-scale continuous deck-girder bridge." Richard Casella and Julian Haas note that Morris Goodkind designed this bridge and oversaw the project, and that the firm of Ash Howard Needles and Tammen (mentioned elsewhere in this book) served as design consultants. Interestingly, these authors also report that only two companies in the United States were capable of fabricating and erecting the necessary steel. Ultimately, the Bethlehem Steel Company won the contract over the American Bridge Company division of the (then named) U.S. Steel Corporation.

At the time of its construction, the Edison Bridge set a record for its three continuous-span girders, which rested on nine spans over the river; overall, the bridge is composed of twenty-nine spans for a total length of 4,391 feet. Today, the nearby Driscoll Bridge carries the Garden State Parkway across the Raritan River. Casella and Haas call it "a nearly identical twin of the Edison Bridge."

SCUDDER FALLS BRIDGE

This otherwise unassuming ten-span bridge with two-span continuous steel-plate girders was built in 1959 but not opened until 1961. Each of its two end spans is 150 feet long, and the eight middle spans are 180 feet each, for a total length of 1,740 feet. A vital link in the Northeast corridor, the bridge carries Interstate 95 across the Delaware River between Ewing Township, New Jersey, and Lower Makefield, Pennsylvania, and crosses over the Pennsylvania Canal on the Pennsylvania side. It replaced a bridge 1.3 miles to the south, between the area known as Wilburtha, on the New Jersey side, and Yardley, Pennsylvania. The present site is piscatorially significant: the relatively rare short-nosed sturgeon swims up from Delaware Bay to spawn in the nontidal waters of Scudder Falls.

One of the refrains of this book has been the importance of the community and environment surrounding each of New Jersey's bridges. A bridge becomes part

SCUDDER FALLS BRIDGE   Representative of modern girder construction, this bridge carries busy Interstate 95 across the Delaware River.

of the history and symbolism of its location, and often its name records an impor- tant, sometimes all but forgotten story. In the case of the Scudder Falls Bridge, the Long Island Genealogy Surname Database identifies a Richard Betts Scudder, who was born in Newtown, Queens County, Long Island, in 1671 and died at "Scudders Falls, Hunterdon County," on March 14, 1754. It appears that this man is the Scud- der for whom the falls were named. The genealogy site traces his ancestry back to Henry Skudder, who was born about 1470 in Kent, England, and married Agnes, also born 1470. The *k* became a *c* in the surname of the Skudders' children. So, when cruising over this highway bridge, we might reflect on a connection reaching back over five centuries to the Middle Ages and Henry and Agnes Skudder in Kent, England. Such is part of the allure of bridges.

The pier structure of Scudder Falls Bridge should be compared with that of the Delaware Water Gap Toll Bridge (color plate 12). That structure's rounded piers, made of granite-reinforced concrete, complement the geology of the Kittatinny Ridge and help the bridge fit aesthetically into the area. Built in 1953 by the Delaware River Joint Toll Bridge Commission, the 2,465-foot, steel-plate girder bridge contains 5,883 tons of steel and 22,550 cubic yards of concrete. The roadways are supported by four steel girders; the westbound north abutment span has five steel rolled beams.

The Delaware Water Gap Toll Bridge is part of the Interstate 80 system at Pahaquarry, New Jersey, and Delaware Water Gap Borough, Pennsylvania. Significantly, it provides a link to the George Washington Bridge, just four miles beyond the other end of Interstate 80 in New Jersey. That highway, which connects San Francisco to New Jersey, was voted one of the worst roads by readers of *Overdrive* magazine in the 1990s, but it seems to have improved at the turn of the twenty-first century. This turnaround is fortunate, for the Delaware Water Gap Toll Bridge brings travelers through one of the most scenic locations in New Jersey. It is also the only bridge in New Jersey that is officially part of the Appalachian Trail, and hikers are allowed to cross it.

CONCLUDING WORDS

More than any other public structure, the bridge is transparent. In the case of most bridges, one can walk or ride over them. Others—railroad freight bridges, for example—can only be viewed. Unlike buildings, whose interiors are often inaccessible except to those who work or conduct business in them, bridges may be observed in their entirety. Especially from a distance, when the perspective of their spans is seen against the landscape, they appear sculptural. As we have seen, they carry symbolic references as well as serve utilitarian purposes. Bridges bind regions politically and economically. A central theme of this book has been the interconnections reflected in bridges, whether a name that reaches back to the Middle Ages, a site that saw action during the American Revolution, or a type of construction that originated in the drawings of a Roman architect.

We live in a world of "instant." Push a button and a picture appears. Hit a key and send an image or message around the world. Buy something, unwrap it, use it up, throw it away, and buy another. We are bombarded by junk mail and spam. No longer do we wait for the news to be delivered at a certain hour; it is available around the clock, and we forget it instantly. We find friendship not in quiet conversation, but vicariously through so-called reality television programming and the lives of celebrities. On a broadly metaphoric level, in photography we are replacing chemicals with photons, moving from the tangible and visible to the intangible and invisible. In short, we have created a temporary world through which we pass fleetingly, our feet barely touching the ground and ourselves barely touching each other.

In this world, these great structures of humankind give us a real, physical reminder of what we are, what we have been, and what we might be. In some places, such as Frogner Park, the showcase for the art of Gustav Vigeland in Oslo, Norway, great works of sculpture present humanity in its various permutations and emotions. In other places, singular monuments, such as the Washington Monument in Washington, D.C., stand as geometric symbols of something else. Engineering feats, such as the Great Wall of China or the pyramids of Egypt, last through the ages as testament to human vision.

The bridge is omnipresent and unique among those feats. Before there is a bridge, there is a vision. It may be a small vision—a small stone arch bridge to traverse a creek—or a large vision—a suspension bridge to cross the Hudson River. In either case, the necessity and vision gave rise to the invention, and the invention became the monument. Bridges are mathematical expressions made tangible. They are among our most noble achievements in the mastery and accommodation of nature. And here in New Jersey, some of the most impressive and significant of these monuments remain to be seen and appreciated.

BIBLIOGRAPHY

I have sought to provide a comprehensive (but not exhaustive) bibliography. The number of books on bridges published over the past seventy-five years is relatively small, and many of the older ones (such as those by Steinman) are still widely used. I have provided sources consulted or, if not expressly consulted, cited by enough other sources to merit inclusion.

A vast amount of information is now available on the Internet. I have listed both general, organizational Web sites and those that offer specific information about a bridge, an engineer, or a bridge company. In addition, some printed sources can be accessed in whole or in part on the Internet; where appropriate, I have given the Web URL.

PRINTED SOURCES

A. G. Lichtenstein and Associates, Inc. September 1994, modified 2001. *The New Jersey Historic Bridge Database.* Prepared for New Jersey Department of Transportation.

———. November 1999. *Contextual Study of New York State's Pre-1961 Bridges.* Prepared for New York State Department of Transportation.

Agnew, Lorraine. 2003. "After Span of 74 Years, Bridge Is Still a Draw." *Courier Post,* 29 August.

Andariese, Walter. 1981. *History of the Benjamin Franklin Bridge.* Camden: Delaware River Port Authority.

Arcila, Martha Torres. 2002. *Bridges.* Mexico City: Atrium.

Avery, Ron. 2001. "The Ben Franklin Bridge—Opened July 1, 1926: One of Our Treasures." *Metro,* 20 June. Posted at http://www.pgwebconsulting.com/boating/pages/Ben_Franklin_Bridge.html (accessed 24 November 2003).

Bascove. 1998. *Stone and Steel: Paintings and Writings Celebrating the Bridges of New York City.* Boston: David R. Godine.

Bennett, David. 1999. *The Creation of Bridges.* London: Quintet Publishing, Inc.

Billington, David P. 1979. *Robert Maillart's Bridges: The Art of Engineering.* Princeton: Princeton University Press.

————. 1985. *The Tower and the Bridge*. Princeton: Princeton, Princeton University Press.

————. 2003. *The Art of Structural Design: A Swiss Legacy*. Princeton: Princeton University Art Museum.

Billington, David P., and F. Gottemoeller. 2000. "Bridge Aesthetics—Structural Art." In *Bridge Engineering Handbook*, edited by Wai-Fah Chen and Lian Duan. Boca Raton, Fla.: CRC Press.

Boothby, Thomas E., et al. 1998. *Stone Arch Bridge Inventory, Phase II*. University Park: Pennsylvania State University. Report submitted to Hunterdon County Planning Board, Flemington, N.J.

Brown, David J. 2001. *Bridges: Three Thousand Years of Defying Nature*. St. Paul: MBI Publishing Co.

Browne, Lionel. 1996. *Bridges: Masterpieces of Architecture*. New York: Todtri Productions Limited.

Brydon, Norman F. 1971. *Of Time, Fire, and the River: The Story of New Jersey's Covered Bridges*. Rev. ed. Essex, N.J.: n.p.

————. 1974. *The Passaic River: Past, Present, and Future*. New Brunswick: Rutgers University Press.

Bush, Laura. 2001. "Delaware Memorial Bridge Set to Turn 50." *The Review* 127, no. 48 (27 April).

Cassella, Richard M., and Julian Haas. 2003. *The History and Technology of the Edison Bridge and Driscoll Bridge over the Raritan River, New Jersey*. [Trenton]: New Jersey Department of Transportation.

Cawley, James, and Margaret Cawley. 1993. *Exploring the Little Rivers of New Jersey*. 4th ed. New Brunswick: Rutgers University Press.

Chatterjee, Sukhen. 1991. *The Design of Modern Steel Bridges*. London: BSP Professional Books.

Chen, Wai-Fah, and Lian Duan, eds. 2000. *Bridge Engineering Handbook*. Boca Raton, Fla.: CRC Press.

Collins, V. Lansing. 1946. *Princeton: Past and Present*. Princeton: Princeton University Press.

Condit, Carl W. 1960. *American Building Art: The Nineteenth Century*. New York: Oxford University Press.

————. 1961. *American Building Art: The Twentieth Century*. New York: Oxford University Press.

Cunningham, John T. 1966. *Newark*. Newark: New Jersey Historical Society.

————. 1966. *New Jersey: America's Main Road*. Garden City, N.Y.: Doubleday and Company.

————. 1999. *This Is New Jersey*. 4th ed. New Brunswick: Rutgers University Press.

D'Agnese, Joseph. 2000. "In Search of the Bridge of Hunterdon County." *New York Times*, sec. 14, p. 4, 25 June.

Dale, Frank T. 2003. *Bridges over the Delaware River: A History of Crossings.* New Brunswick: Rutgers University Press.

Darnell, Victor C. 1984. *Directory of American Bridge Building Companies 1840–1900.* Washington, D.C.: Society for Industrial Archeology.

"David Fine, Engineer, Dies at 85." 1980. *New York Times,* sec. B, p. 15, 15 September.

Delaware River Joint Toll Bridge Commission. 1995. *General Information on the Non-Toll Bridges.* N.p.

———. 1996. *General Information on Toll Bridges.* N.p. (See also http://www.drjtbc.com.)

DeLeuw, Cather and Company, and Engineering-Science, Inc. 1991. New Jersey Transit Railroad Bridge Survey. Prepared for New Jersey Transit, New Jersey Department of Environmental Protection.

DeLony, Eric. 1992. *Landmark American Bridges.* Boston: Little Brown and Company.

Del Vecchio, Mike. 2001. *Pictorial History of America's Railroads.* Osceola, Wis.: MBI Publishing Company.

Doherty, C. H. 1969. *Bridges.* New York: Meredith Press.

Dorwart, Jeffrey. 2001. *Camden County, New Jersey: The Making of a Metropolitan Community, 1626–2000.* New Brunswick: Rutgers University Press.

Driscoll v. Burlington-Bristol Bridge Co. 8 N.J. 433 (1952).

Dupré, Judith. 1997. *Bridges: A History of the World's Most Famous and Important Spans.* New York: Black Dog and Leventhal Publishers.

Encyclopedia of New Jersey. 2004. Edited by Maxine N. Lurie and Marc Mappen. New Brunswick: Rutgers University Press.

Evans, Benjamin D., and June R. Evans. 2001. *Pennsylvania's Covered Bridges.* 2nd ed. Pittsburgh: University of Pittsburgh Press.

Flint, Anthony. 1997. "Some Highlights in the History of Bridge Design." In *Structural Engineering: History and Development,* edited by R.J.W. Milne. London: E&FN Spon.

Freeland, Cynthia. 2001. *But Is It Art?* Oxford: Oxford University Press.

"Gen. Goethals Dies After Long Illness." 1928. *New York Times,* 22 January.

Gies, Joseph. 1963. *Bridges and Men.* Garden City, N.Y.: Doubleday and Company.

———. 1966. *Wonders of the Modern World: Thirteen Great Achievements of Modern Engineering.* New York: Thomas Y. Crowell Company.

Gillespie, Angus Kress, and Michael Aaron Rockland. 1989. *Looking for America on the New Jersey Turnpike.* New Brunswick: Rutgers University Press.

Gordon, J. E. 1978. *Structures: Or Why Things Don't Fall Down.* New York: Da Capo Press.

Gorenstein, Nathan. 1994. "Span Still Over Troubled Economic Waters." *Philadelphia Inquirer,* 1 February.

Gottemoeller, Frederick. 1998. *Bridgescape: The Art of Designing Bridges.* New York: John Wiley and Sons.

Graf, Bernhard. 2002. *Bridges That Changed the World*. Munich: Prestel.

Griggs, Francis E., Jr. 2003. "Niagara Cantilever." *Journal of Bridge Engineering* 8, no. 1 (January–February): 2–11.

Harris, David W. 1999. *Truss Fun*. Lakewood, Colo.: BaHa Enterprises.

"Henry Balke, Bridge Builder, Dies." 1980. *New York Times*, 29 November.

Hewitt, Louise. 1916. *Historic Trenton*. Trenton: Smith Press.

Höcker, Christoph. 2000. *Architecture: An Illustrated Overview*. New York: Barron's Educational Services.

Hokanson, Drake. 1988. *The Lincoln Highway: Main Street Across America*. Iowa City: University of Iowa Press.

Holgate, Alan. 1986. *The Art in Structural Design*. Oxford: Oxford University Press. Available online at http://home.vicnet.net.au/~aholgate/structdes/taisd/_anchor.html (accessed 3 July 2003).

Hopkins, H. J. 1970. *A Span of Bridges: An Illustrated History*. New York: Praeger Publishers.

Jackson, Donald C. 1984. *Great American Bridges and Dams*. New York: John C. Wiley and Sons.

Jacobs, David, and Anthony E. Neville. 1968. *Bridges, Canals & Tunnels*. New York: American Heritage Publishing Company.

John A. Roebling: An Account at the Unveiling of a Monument to His Memory. 1908. N.p.: Roebling Press.

Johnson, Stephen, and Robert T. Leon. 2002. *Encyclopedia of Bridges and Tunnels*. New York: Checkmark Books.

Ketchum, Robert M. 1973. *The Winter Soldiers*. Garden City, N.Y.: Doubleday and Company.

Kirby, Richard Shelton, et al. [1956] 1990. *Engineering in History*. Mineola, N.Y.: Dover Publications.

Koughan, James. 1996. "The Collapse of the Tacoma Narrows Bridge: Evaluation of Competing Theories of Its Demise, and the Effects of Disaster on Succeeding Bridge Designs." University of Texas at Austin, Department of Mechanical Engineering. *Undergraduate Engineering Review*.

Lane, Wheaton J. 1939. *From Indian Trail to Iron Horse: Travel and Transportation in New Jersey, 1620–1860*. Princeton: Princeton University Press.

Leonhardt, Fritz. 1984. *Bridges: Aesthetics and Design*. Cambridge, Mass.: MIT Press.

———. 1997. "Reflections on 60 Years of Structural Development." In *Structural Engineering: History and Development*, edited by R.J.W. Milne. London: E&FN Spon.

Macaulay, David. 2000. *Building Big*. Boston: Houghton Mifflin Company. (See also http://www.pbs.org/wgbh/buildingbig.)

McCullough, David. 1972. *The Great Bridge: The Epic Story of the Building of the Brooklyn Bridge*. New York: Simon and Schuster.

McGraw-Hill Encyclopedia of Science & Technology. 1987. 6th ed. New York: McGraw-Hill Book Company.

Middleton, William D. 1999. *Landmarks on the Iron Road.* Bloomington and Indianapolis: Indiana University Press.

Milne, R.J.W., ed. 1997. *Structural Engineering: History and Development.* London: E&FN Spon.

Mock, Elizabeth. 1949. *The Architecture of Bridges.* New York: Museum of Modern Art.

"Modjeski, Ralph." 2003. In *Biography Resource Center.* Farmington Hills, Mich.: Gale Group.

Myers, William Starr, ed. 1945. *The Story of New Jersey.* New York: Lewis Historical Publishing Company.

Mysak, Joe, and Judith Schiffer. 1997. *Perpetual Motion: The Illustrated History of the Port Authority of New York and New Jersey.* New York: General Publishing Group.

Newberry, Lida, ed. 1977. *New Jersey: A Guide to Its Present and Past.* 2nd rev. ed. New York: Hastings House.

Newhouse, Elizabeth L., ed. 1992. *The Builders: Marvels of Engineering.* Washington, D.C.: National Geographic Society.

New York Times. 1973. Abstract regarding Commodore Barry Bridge. 16 December.

Ochshorn, Jonathan. 2003. "Truss Systems in 20th-Century Architecture." In *Encyclopedia of Twentieth-Century Architecture.* New York: Fitzroy Dearborn. Online at http://people.cornell.edu/pages/jo24/comments/truss.html (accessed 27 November 2003). Related articles on bridge materials by the same author can be found at this site.

Ostrow, Steven A. 1997. *Bridges.* New York: Michael Friedman Publishing Group.

Paine. Thomas. [1803] 1908. "The Construction of Iron Bridges." In *The Life and Writings of Thomas Paine,* ed. Daniel Edwin Wheeler. New York: Vincent Parke and Company. Online at http://socserv2.socsci.mcmaster.ca/~econ/ugcm/3ll3/paine/volume10/236-248%20The%20Construction%20of%20Iron%20Bridges.rtf (accessed 25 January 2004).

Palladio, Andrea. [1570] 1997. *The Four Books on Architecture,* trans. Robert Tavenor and Richard Schofield. Cambridge, Mass., and London: MIT Press.

Petroski, Henry. 1985. *To Engineer Is Human: The Role of Failure in Successful Design.* New York: St. Martin's Press.

———. 1995. *Engineers of Dreams: Great Bridge Builders and the Spanning of America.* New York: Alfred A. Knopf.

———. 1997. *Invention by Design.* Cambridge, Mass.: Harvard University Press.

Phoenix Bridge Company. 1885. *Album of Designs of the Phoenix Bridge Company.* . . . Philadelphia: J. B. Lippincott. Online at http://bridges.lib.lehigh.edu/books/book 1621.html (accessed 18 September 2003).

Plowden, David. 1974. *Bridges: The Spans of North America.* New York: Viking Press.

Pope, Thomas. 1811. *A Treatise on Bridge Architecture.* . . . New York: printed for the author by A. Niven. Online at http://bridges.lib.lehigh.edu/books/book1601.html (accessed 27 November 2003).

Rastorfer, Darl. 2000. *Six Bridges: The Legacy of Othmar H. Ammann.* New Haven: Yale University Press.

"Reaching to the Crescent City: New Orleans Jazzes Up the Cantilever-Truss." 1984. *Engineering News Record*, 26 April.

Reddan, Frank A. "Longest of Its Kind in the World." Typescript, n.d. On file at the New Jersey State Library (J388.1 R313).

Reier, Sharon. 1977. *The Bridges of New York.* Mineola, N.Y.: Dover Publications.

Reifer, Jodi Lee. 1999. "P.A. Still Considering Goethals Bridge Twin." *Staten Island Advance*, 19 October.

Roberts, Russell. 1995. *Discover the Hidden New Jersey.* New Brunswick: Rutgers University Press.

Sayenga, Donald. 1983. *Ellet and Roebling.* York, Pa.: American Canal and Transportation Center.

Schodek, Daniel L. 1988. *Landmarks in American Civil Engineering.* Cambridge, Mass.: MIT Press.

Schuyler, Hamilton. [1931] 1978. *The Roeblings: A Century of Engineers, Bridgebuilders, and Industrialists.* Princeton: Princeton University Press.

"Secrets of the Master Builders: Creating the Impossible in Stone and Steel." 2003. Special issue of *U.S. News and World Report.*

Sev, Aysin. 2001. "Integrating Architecture and Structural Form in Tall Steel Building Design." *CTBUH Review* 1, no. 2 (February). Online at http://www.ctbuh.org/journal/iprev.htm.

Shank, William H. 1980. *Historic Bridges of Pennsylvania.* York, Pa.: American Canal and Transportation Center.

Shapiro, Mary J. 1983. *A Picture History of the Brooklyn Bridge.* New York: Dover Publications.

Shuman, Eleanore Nolan. 1958. *The Trenton Story.* Trenton: MacCrellish and Quigley Company.

Slaughter, Alan R. 2000. "The Preservation and Restoration of Georgian Court Bridge." *Bridge Builder Magazine* (March/April).

Sloane, Eric. [1954] 2002. *American Barns and Covered Bridges.* Mineola, N.Y.: Dover Publications.

Stansfield, Charles A., Jr. 1998. *A Geography of New Jersey.* 2nd ed. New Brunswick: Rutgers University Press.

Steinman, David B. 1945. *The Builders of the Bridge: The Story of John Roebling and His Son.* New York: Harcourt, Brace and Company.

Steinman, David B., and Sara Ruth Watson. 1941. *Bridges and Their Builders.* New York: G. P. Putnam's Sons.

Sutherland, Cara A. 2003. *Portraits of America: Bridges of New York City.* New York: Barnes and Noble Publishing.

Talese, Gay. [1964] 2003. *The Bridge.* New York: Walker and Company.

"Thomas Pope's Flying Bridge: An Incident of Ancient History Revived." 1890. *The Manufacturer and Builder: A Practical Journal of Industrial Design* 22, no. 3 (March): 60. Online at Cornell University Library, Making of America. http://cdl.library.cornell.edu/cgi-bin/moa/sgml/moa-idx?notisid=ABS1821-0022-160 (accessed 27 November 2003).

Tonias, Demetrios E. 1995. *Bridge Engineering.* New York: McGraw-Hill.

Viteri, Maria. 2002. "Beating the Learning Curve—Arches Are In." *Masonry Magazine* (September). Online at http://www.masonrymagazine.com/9-02/cover.html.

Waddell, J.A.L. 1884. *The Designing of Ordinary Iron Highway Bridges.* New York: J. Wiley. Online at http://bridges.lib.lehigh.edu/books/book2311.html (accessed 5 October 2003).

Walker, Edwin Robert, et al. 1929. *A History of Trenton (1679–1929).* Princeton: Princeton University Press.

Wells, Matthew. 2002. *30 Bridges.* New York: Watson-Guptill Publications.

Whipple, Squire. 1869. *Bridge-building.* Albany, N.Y.: n.p. Online at http://bridges.lib.lehigh.edu/books/book2301.html (accessed 5 October 2003).

———. 1899. *An Elementary and Practical Treatise on Bridge Building.* 2nd ed. rev. New York: Van Nostrand. Online at http://bridges.lib.lehigh.edu/books/book2351.html (accessed 5 October 2003).

Whitman, Walt. [1892] 1995. *Specimen Days & Collect.* New York: Dover Publications.

Whitney, Charles S. [1929] 2003. *Bridges of the World: Their Design and Construction.* Mineola, N.Y.: Dover Publications.

Wolfe, Uriah. 1996. "The Need for Aesthetics in Civil Engineering." Technical Communication Program, Department of Engineering Professional Development, University of Wisconsin–Madison, *Undergraduate Engineering Review.* Online at http://elvis.engr.wisc.edu/uer/uer96/author4/content.hmtl (accessed 3 July 2003).

Woodward, Major E. M., and John F. Hageman. 1883. "Princeton." Chapter 42 of *History of Burlington and Mercer Counties, New Jersey.* Philadelphia: Everts and Peck. Online at http://www.rootsweb.com/~njmercer/Mun/PrinTHis.htm (accessed 7 September 2003).

The WPA Guide to 1930s New Jersey. [1939] 1986. New Brunswick: Rutgers University Press.

Zuchowski, Dave. 2003. "Covered Bridge Festival Rumbles into 33rd Year." *Pittsburgh Post-Gazette*, 14 September. Online at http://www.pittsburghpostgazette.com/neigh_washington/20030914wabridge6.asp (accessed 2 October 2003).

INTERNET RESOURCES

American Bridge Company. http://www.americanbridge.net.

American Institute of Steel Construction. www.aisc.org.

American Society of Civil Engineers. "History and Heritage of Civil Engineering: Northampton Street Bridge." http://www.asce.org/history/brdg_northampton.html.

———. "Lehigh Valley History." http://sections.asce.org/lehigh/History.htm.

Anderson, Steve. New Jersey/New York crossings. www.nycroads.com.

———. New Jersey/Pennsylvania crossings. www.phillyroads.com.

Barnicle, Don, and Paula Williams. "Touring the Lackawanna Cutoff." www.njskylands.com/hscutoff.htm.

Behl, Dan, et al. "The Tacony-Palmyra Bridge." Cited at www.phillyroads.com/crossings/tacony-palmyra (accessed 19 June 2003).

Bell, William Gardner. "James Madison Porter." U.S. Army, Center of Military History. http://www.army.mil/cmh-pg/books/sw-sa/PorterJM.htm (accessed 18 September 2003).

Besterfield, Glen H. "Annotated Links to Web Sites on Bascule Bridges." University of South Florida, College of Engineering. http://www.eng.usf.edu/~besterfi/bascule/links_to_web_sites_on_bascule_br.htm.

Billington, David P. 2002. Interview for the "Bridging New York" segment of *Great Projects: The Building of America*. www.pbs.org/greatprojects/interviews/billington_1.html (accessed 25 January 2004).

Branch Brook Park Alliance. http://www.branchbrookpark.org.

Brantacan. Private Web site "concerned with human constructions," especially bridges. www.brantacan.co.uk.

Bridgeman. Private Web site with a bridge chronology and bridge dictionary. http://www.nireland.com/bridgeman.

BridgePros LLC. "BridgePros . . . Dedicated to the Engineering, History, and Construction of Bridges." http://bridgepros.com.

Burlington County Bridge Commission. www.bcbridges.org.

Burlington County Library System. "The County Bridges." www.burlco.lib.nj.us/county/history/bridges.html.

Butler, Howard Russell. "A Short History of Princeton's Rowing Facilities." www.princeton.edu/~crew/features/butler_papers.html.

Chesler, Caren. "NJ Transit Sees Future in the Past." http://flatrock.org.nz/topics/new_jersey/nj_transit_sees_future_in_past.htm.

Coulter, Douglas. "Iron Bridges." http://douglascoulter.com/BridgeSigns/iron_bridges.html (accessed 5 October 2003).

Cridlebaugh, Bruce S. "Bridges and Tunnels of Allegheny County and Pittsburgh, Pa." http://pghbridges.com.

Delaware Department of Transportation. "Delaware's Historic Bridges." www.deldot. net/static/projects/archaeology/historic_pres/delaware/bridge_book/bridge_toc. html (accessed 24 January 2004).

Delaware River and Bay Authority. www.drba.net.

Delaware River Port Authority. www.drpa.com.

Denenberg, David. "A Span for All Seasons." www.bridgemeister.com.

Drew, Thomas. 2000. "Engineered Art." Technical Communication Program, Department of Engineering Professional Development, University of Wisconsin–Madison. http://tc.engr.wisc.edu/Steuber/papers/2000/Bridge.doc (accessed 24 January 2004).

Easton, Pennsylvania. "A Brief History and Architectural Tour." http://easton-pa.com/ History/HistoricEaston.htm (accessed 19 March 2000).

Elizabeth, New Jersey. "Goethals Bridge." http://www.elizabethnj.org/factsGoethals Bridge.htm (accessed 3 March 2000).

Fairfield University, Mathematics Department. "Geometry of Bridge Construction." www.faculty.fairfield.edu/jmac/rs/bridges.htm (accessed 25 January 2004).

Fekete, Tom. "The Ben Franklin Bridge and the Waterfront." http://www.maplecherry. org/bridge.html.

Fort Lee Online. "George Washington Bridge." http://www.fortleeonline.com/gwb (accessed 21 July 2003).

Gambardello, Joseph A. 2003. "Rare Bridges to the Past." *Philadelphia Inquirer*. www. philly.com/mld/inquirer/6505584.htm (posted 11 August 2003).

Garden State Model Railway Club, Inc. "The Great Lackawanna Cutoff—Then & Now." www.gsmrrclub.org/HISTORY/history5.html

Garvin, James L. "History of the Depot or Meadow Bridge." http://www.shelburnenh. com/bridge.html (accessed 19 January 2004).

Gauvreau, Paul. "Bridge Aesthetics." University of Toronto, Faculty of Applied Science and Engineering. www.ecf.utoronto.ca/apsc/courses/civ356/bridge_aesthetics. htm (accessed 4 July 2003).

———. "The Three Myths of Bridge Aesthetics." University of Toronto, Faculty of Applied Science and Engineering. www.ecf.utoronto.ca/apsc/courses/civ356/3%20 Myths%2002%2005%2023%202.pdf (accessed 24 January 2004).

Georgian Court University. "About Georgian Court." http://www.georgian.edu/ aboutgcc/gould.htm (accessed 6 September 2003).

Gilgenbach, Cara, and Paul Gregor. "Erie Lackawanna Railroad Inventory: Historical Note." University of Akron Archival Services. http://www3.uakron.edu/archival/ ErieLack/Hist.htm (accessed 9 September 2003).

Golia, Michael. "Geometry of Bridges." Yale–New Haven Teachers Institute. http:// www.yale.edu/ynhti/curriculum/units/2001/5/01.05.09.x.html (accessed 12 October 2003).

Graciano Corporation. "Georgian Court Bridge." http://www.graciano.com/georgian. htm (accessed 6 September 2003).

Green, Perry S. "Historic Bridge Home Page." University of Florida, Department of Civil and Coastal Engineering. www.ce.ufl.edu/~historic (accessed 19 March 2000).

Guest Services, Inc. "New Jersey's Great Northwest Skylands." http://www.njskylands. com.

Gupta, Ashok, and Sachin Dhir. "Internet Knowledge Base for Bridge Engineering." Indian Institute of Technology Delhi, Department of Civil Engineering. http://www.ncst.ernet.in/vidyakash/online-content/webiit/bridge/homepagedes.htm (accessed 21 December 2003).

Hardesty & Hanover LLP. http://hardesty-hanover.com (accessed 25 July 2004).

Historical Society of Delaware. "The Delaware Memorial Bridge." http://www.hsd.org/ DHE/DHE_where_transport_DMB.htm (accessed 24 December 2003).

"Historical Timeline of Concrete." Auburn University. http://www.auburn.edu/academic/architecture/bsc/classes/bsc314/timeline/timeline.htm (accessed 21 December 2003).

Historic American Buildings Survey/Historic American Engineering Record. http://www.cr.nps.gov/habshaer.

Homasote Company. "About the Homasote Company—Company History." http://www.pakline.com/about/history.html (accessed 2 October 2003).

Hunterdon County, New Jersey. "Hunterdon County's Stone Arch Bridges." http://www.co.hunterdon.nj.us/stone (accessed 31 December 2003).

———. "Stockton Borough History." http://www.co.hunterdon.nj.us/mun/stockton/history.htm (accessed 30 November 2003).

iCivilEngineer. "Famous Engineers." www.icivilengineer.com/Famous_Engineers.

Invention Factory. "John Roebling's Sons Co.: Online History Archive." http://www.inventionfactory.com/history/main.html.

Jayachandran, P. "Structural Engineering: A Historical Perspective." Worcester Polytechnic Institute, Department of Civil and Environmental Engineering. cee.wpi.edu/ce1030_b02/structures/history.pdf (accessed 25 January 2004).

Jersey City Past and Present. "General Casimir Pulaski Memorial Skyway." New Jersey City University. www.njcu.edu/programs/jchistory/Pages/P_Pages/Pulaski_Skyway.htm (accessed 23 January 2004).

"The King Bridge Company Museum." http://www.kingbridgecompany.com (accessed 13 January 2004).

Kingston Greenways Association. "Kingston: Crossroads to History 1675– ." www. kingstongreenways.org.history.html (accessed 6 July 2003).

Lake Carnegie Construction Photographs. Historical Photograph Collection, Department of Rare Books and Special Collections, Princeton University Library. http://libweb.princeton.edu/libraries/firestone/rbsc/finding_aids/carnegie.html (accessed 7 September 2003).

Lehigh University Libraries. "Digital Bridges: Bridges of the Nineteenth Century: A Twenty-first Century Book Collection." http://bridges.lib.lehigh.edu/index.html.

"Lenticular Truss Bridges" http://explorer.road.jp/bridges/lenticulartruss/index-e.html (accessed 4 July 2003).

Lincoln Highway Association. "The Lincoln Highway in New York and New Jersey." www.lincolnhighwayassoc.org/info/ny-nj.

Lutenegger, Alan J., and Amy B. Cerato. "Lenticular Truss Bridges of Massachusetts." University of Massachusetts, Department of Civil and Environmental Engineering. http://www.ecs.umass.edu/cee/cee_web/bridge/1.html.

Maryland State Highway Administration. "Historic Highway Bridges in Maryland: 1631–1960." www.sha.state.md.us/keepingcurrent/maintainRoadsBridges/bridges/OPPE/historicBridges/histbrpg0.asp (accessed 18 January 2004).

McCain, Roger A. "Green Sergeant's Covered Bridge." http://william-king.www.drexel.edu/top/bridge/CBGS.HTML (accessed 14 September 2003).

McElney, Brian. "The Primacy of Chinese Inventions." Bath Royal Literary and Scientific Institution. http://www.brlsi.org/proceed02/science017.htm (accessed 24 November 2003).

Mercer County, New Jersey. "Mercer County History—PRR Bridge." http://www.rootsweb.com/~njmercer/Site/PRRbridge.htm.

Morrissey, Michael. "How Bridges Work." HowStuffWorks, Inc. http://travel.howstuffworks.com/bridges.htm (accessed 25 January 2004).

Multnomah County, Oregon. "Multnomah County Bridges." http://www.multnomah.lib.or.us/bridge.

Musser, Josh. "Ironhorse Image Gallery." http://www.geocities.com/ironhorseusa2000.

Nadler, Jerrold. "Rebuilding the Port of New York." Five Borough Institute. http://www.fiveborough.org/5boroughreport/nadler_tunnel.html (accessed 2 October 2003).

Nansi, B. P. "Let Us Build Bridges." 2001. Project Monitor, Economic Research India Limited. http://www.projectsmonitor.com/detailnews.asp?newsid=3161 (posted 1 December 2001; accessed 21 December 2001).

National Concrete Bridge Council. "Concrete Advantage." http://www.national-concretebridge.org/advantage.html (accessed 25 November 2003).

National Museum of Science and Technology, Milan. "Leonardo da Vinci—Revolving Bridge." http://www.museoscienza.org/english/leonardo/pontegirevole.html (accessed 23 November 2003).

National Register of Historic Places. www.nationalregisterofhistoricplaces.com.

New Jersey Department of Transportation. www.state.nj.us/transportation.

New Jersey Historic Trust. "Georgian Court Bridge." www.njht.org.profiles/georgian-court-bridge.html.

New Jersey Network. "Bridges" segment of Life 360. http://www.njn.net/television/specials/life360/themesbridges.html (accessed 19 July 2003).

New Jersey Society of Professional Engineers, Mercer County Chapter. "History." http://www.njspe.org/Mercer3.htm (accessed 2 October 2003).

Nicolas Janberg Internet Content Services. "Structurae." www.structurae.de.

Oliveto, Gerald. "Gerald's Railroads of New Jersey: Movable Railroad Bridges of New Jersey." www.geocities.com/transit383/bridges.html.

Outerbridge, Thomas. "The Infrastructure to Replace Fresh Kills." Letter to *Staten Island Advance*, 8 December 1999. Posted by City Green, Inc. http://www.citygreen.net/commentary.htm (accessed 2 October 2003).

"Pennsylvania's Historic Architecture and Archaelogy." www.arch.state.pa.us.

Philadelphia Architects and Buildings Project. "Pennsylvania Railroad Delaware River Bridge." www.philadelphiabuildings.org/pab/app/pj_display.cfm/19840.

Polish American Cultural Center. "Ralph Modjeski (1861–1940)." http://www.polish-americancenter.org/Modjeski.htm (accessed 24 November 2003).

Port Authority of New York and New Jersey. http://www.panynj.gov.

Princeton Township. "1996 Princeton Community Master Plan: Historic Preservation Element." www.princetontwp.org/masterplan/mphistpres.html.

Princeton Township Historic Preservation Commission. "Historic Preservation in Princeton Township: A Brief History of Princeton." www.princetontwp.org/histofpt.html.

Public Archaeology Survey Team, Inc. "Connecticut's Historic Highway Bridges." http://www.past-inc.org/historic-bridges.

Public Broadcasting System, WGBH, Boston. 12 November 1997. *NOVA*. "Super Bridge." Transcript. http://www.pbs.org/wgbh/nova/transcripts/2416bridge.html.

———. 29 February 2000. *NOVA*. "Secrets of Lost Empires: China Bridge." Transcript. http://www.pbs.org/wgbh/nova/transcripts/27fbchina.html (accessed 24 November 2003).

Raub, Janet. "Phillipsburg, New Jersey: Charter Jubilee." http://raub-and-more.com/pburgcharterjubilee/history.html (accessed 2 October 2003).

"The Remaining Covered Bridges of West Virginia." http://members.citynet.net/post (accessed 5 October 2003).

Rice University, Department of Civil and Environmental Engineering. "The Bridges Project." http://128.42.22.5/scripts/bridges/front_end/welcome.asp?opennew=2& images=1.

Ritter, Michael A. 1990. "Timber as a Bridge Material." Chapter 1 of *Timber Bridges: Design, Construction, Inspection and Maintenance*. United States Department of Agriculture, Forest Service. www.fs.fed.us/na/wit/pdf/timberbridgespub/WIT-02-0001.ch1.pdf (accessed 25 January 2004).

Smith, John D. "When Trains Had Names." www.njskylands.com/hstrains.htm.

Smith, William. "Pons." 1875. *Dictionary of Greek and Roman Antiquities*. www.ukans. edu/history/index/europe/ ancient_rome/E/Roman/Texts/Secondary/SMIGRA/ Pons.html (accessed 25 January 2004).

"Streets of Camden, NJ" (Federal Street and State Street). Delaware Valley Rhythm & Blues Society, Inc. http://www.dvrbs.com/CandenNJ-Streets-FederalStreet.htm and -StateStreet.htm (accessed 11 January 2004).

Suyolcu, Yavuz. "New Bridge Design: Structural and Artistic Concepts." Middle East Technical University. http://vision1.eee.metu.edu.tr/~metafor/yazi/1125bridge. html (accessed 24 January 2004).

Taher, Rima. "The Art of Structural Bridge Design." American Society of Civil Engineers, North Jersey Branch. http://branches.asce.org/northjersey/techgroups/ Structural/The%20Art%20of%20Bridge%20Design.pdf (accessed 24 January 2004).

———. "Bridges: Structural Systems and Design, Fall 2002." New Jersey Institute of Technology. web.njit.edu/~taher/Bridges.pdf (accessed 25 January 2004).

Talese, Gay. 2002. Interview for the "Bridging New York" segment of *Great Projects: The Building of America*. www.pbs.org/greatprojects/interviews/talese_1.html (accessed 25 January 2004).

Tennessee Department of Transportation. "A Brief History of Covered Bridges in Tennessee." www.tdot.state.tn.us/bridges/historybridges.htm.

"Uhlerstown Village and Rural Historic District." The Gombach Group. http://www. livingplaces.net/pa/bucks/historicdistricts/uhlerstown/uhlerstownhistdist.html (accessed 30 November 2003).

University of Manchester Institute of Science and Technology. "Bridges." http://www. umist.ac.uk/construction/intranet/teaching/ue365/lectures/bridges.htm (accessed 5 October 2003).

Viau, Robert. "Vitruvius & Palladio." http://www.faculty.de.gcsu.edu/~rviau/ids/Artworks/neoclassical.html (accessed 22 November 2003).

Weird New Jersey. "Weird Wonders of NJ: The Paulinskill Viaduct," www.weirdnj.com/ _abandoned/paulinskill.html.

WHYY (Philadelphia). "Ben Franklin Bridge" segment of *Secrets Beneath the Streets*. http://www.whyy.org/tv12/secrets/bfb.html (accessed 24 November 2003).

Wortley Top Forge Industrial Museum. "Glossary of Iron Working Names and Terms." http://www.topforge.co.uk/Glossary.htm (accessed 25 November 2003).

WQED (Pittsburgh). "Pittsburgh History Series Teachers' Guide: Structure: Defying Gravity." http://www.wqed.org/erc/pghist/units/build/structure1.shtml (accessed 21 July 2003).

PATENTS

Ash, Louis R. Center Lock for Bascule Bridges. Patent 1,646,340. 18 October 1927.

Douglas, William O. Improvement in Truss Bridges. Patent 202,526. 16 April 1878.

BIBLIOGRAPHY

Howe, William. Truss-Frame for Bridges. Patent 1,685. 10 July 1840.

———. Manner of Constructing the Truss-Frames of Bridges and Other Structures. Patent 1,711. 3 August 1840, reissued 3 September 1850.

———. Truss-Bridge. Patent 4,726. 28 August 1846.

INDEX

ABOUT THE AUTHOR

Steven M. Richman, J.D., is an adjunct professor of international business law at the College of New Jersey, and an attorney in private practice. He received a B.A. from Drew University and a J.D. from New York University. His publications include contributions to *The Encyclopedia of New Jersey* (Rutgers University Press), *New Jersey Federal Civil Practice* (New Jersey Law Journal Books), and *American Poetry Confronts the 90s* (Black Tie Press). His photography is in public and private collections.